Wire
Jewelry
WORKSHOP

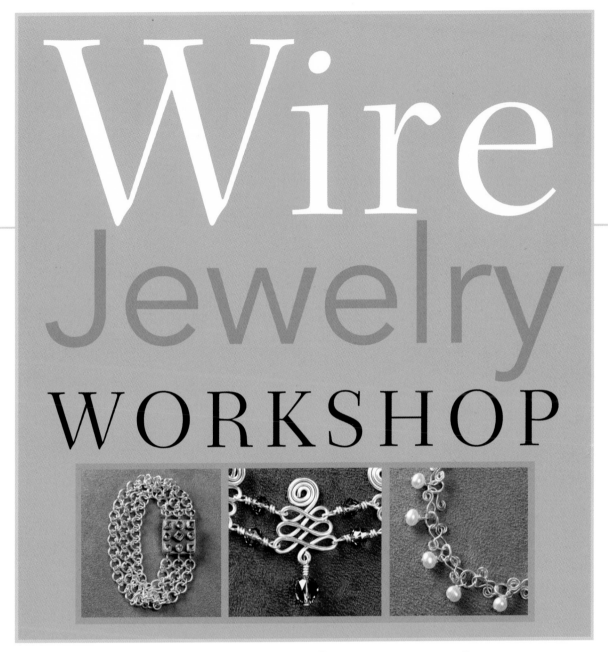

Techniques for Working With Wire and Beads

SUSAN RAY

©2008 Susan Ray
Published by

kp **krause publications**
An Imprint of F+W Publications

700 East State Street • Iola, WI 54990-0001
715-445-2214 • 888-457-2873
www.krausebooks.com

Our toll-free number to place an order or obtain a free catalog is (800) 258-0929.

NOTE: These instructions are made available for your entertainment and enjoyment.
They are not intended for commercial use.

American Wire Gauge; Arrow Springs Glass; Art Jewelry®, Artistic Wire, Ltd.™; Bali Beads, Badger® Balm; Bead and Button®; Bead Appreciation; Bead Stoppers; BeadStyle®; Beadalon®; Beadazzled, Inc.®; Beadazzled, Where Beads and Inspiration Meet; Beadwork®; Cas Webber Photography; Copper Loom; Delica®; Dichroic; Dremel®; E6000® Glue, Earthstone.com; Ebb Designs; Fiber Optic Beads; Firemountain Gems and Beads®; Flecto®; Frantz Art Glass & Supply; Galena Beads "serving creativity"; Google™; Griffin Silk™; G-S Hypo™ Tube Cement; Hot Pot; Hot Stuff Special "T"™ Illusion Glue; Knot Just Beads®; Krylon®; Lapidary Journal®; Liver of Sulphur; Memory Wire, Miracle Beads, National Geographic Society; National Public Radio; NuGold, Nymo® Thread; Polarfleece®; Rio Grande; Riverstone Beads; Rolo Chain, Swarovski® Crystal Beads; Shutterfly; Soft Flex, Soft Touch; Sculpey® Super Flex; Super Glue®; Teflon®; The Bead Museum, Washington, DC; The Bead Society of Greater Washington; Coiling Gizmo®, Professional Deluxe Gizmo, Econo Winder and Deluxe Gizmo; The History of Beads, by Lois Durbin; Vintaj Natural Brass Co.™; Wig Jig® Centaur, Cyclops and Delphi; William L. Allen; X-acto

Library of Congress Catalog Number: 2007939098
ISBN: 13: 978-0-89689-668-0
ISBN: 10: 0-89689-668-4
Edited by: Shelley Coffman
Designed by: Dana Boll, BookBuster Publishing Services
Printed in China

Wire Jewelry

Jewelry

WORKSHOP

Techniques for Working With Wire and Beads

SUSAN RAY

DEDICATION

for Eric,

…because you are mine,
always.

Acknowledgments

I would like to thank the following people for their individual contributions in bringing this book to life:

- Juli Ikonomopoulos, whose talents and patience make every task easier. Thank you for being a partner in this enormous undertaking and your dedication and friendship.
- Cas Webber, for her design talent and her enthusiasm, and the delectable photographics of the talented designers of Beadazzled.
- Sue Wilke, for always giving so generously.
- Candy Wiza, Krause Publications' acquisition editor, who lets me "garden." Your talents, collaboration and creativity are remarkable.
- Krause Publications and F+W Publications, for their continued and gracious latitude.
- Dana Boll, Bookbuster Publishing Services, for her creativity to set every page with such an artful eye.

- Kris Kandler and Lynn Mann-Hallmark, for the Krause Publications' studio photography gracing so many of these pages insightfully.
- LeRoy Goertz, once again, for his informative and skilled techniques with the Coiling Gizmo.
- Gary Helwig, for giving us your time, talent and skills both on and off of the WigJig.
- Trish Italia, Jan Ketza Harris, and Jessica Italia (and the rest of the bead divas) of Galena Beads, for "serving creativity" 24/7.
- Wendy Mullane, Jeanne Holland, and Jessica Italia of Vintaj Natural Brass Co., for sharing their love of vintage findings and reviving their use almost single-handedly.

- The creative designs of so many wonderfully talented jewelry designers: Ilene Baranowitz, Sherrie Chapin, LeRoy Goertz, Gary Helwig, Darien Kaiser, Jan Ketza Harris, Jeanne Holland, Jessica Italia, Trish Italia, Susan A. Karczewski, Deanna and Janet Killackey, Sue Kwong and Karen Li, Dotsie S. Mack, Kathleen Manning, Barbara Markoe, Mackenzie Mullane, Wendy Mullane, Patrick Ober, Cathie Roberts, Megan Starkey, Ronda Terry, Cas K. Webber, Sandi Webster, and Sue Wilke.
- Kat Allison and Cindy Yost, for sharing their creative talents at creating bead landscapes on their very resourceful loom.
- Eric Petersen, for his council and conservation.
- Chris Baker, for sharing her beautiful B&B, Mont Rest, in Bellevue, Iowa when I needed to rest the most.
- J.B., honestly, every day something you taught me comes to mind. My thanks for being in my life.
- Kevin, for all else.

NOTE: All jewelry is measured without clasps. All earrings are measured dangles only, without ear wire. If you use a different clasp or ear wire, your finished size will change. To increase the length, add more beads. To decrease length, remove a few beads. Always measure twice and crimp once.

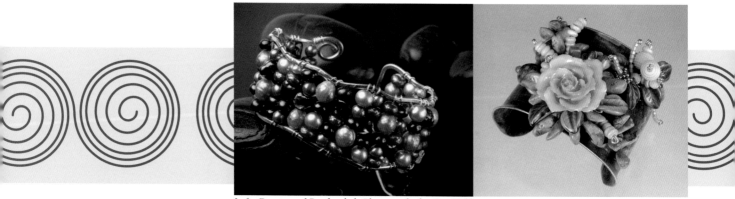

Left: Courtesy of Beadazzled. Photography by Cas Webber.
Right: Courtesy of Sandra Webster: Copper Cuff.

Courtesy of Barbara Markoe: Noe Lani Bracelet.

Table of Contents

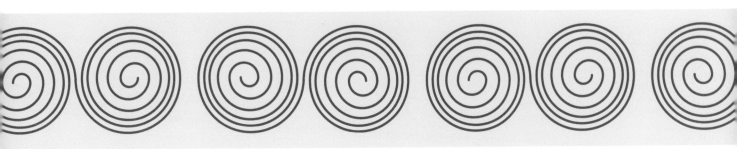

Courtesy of Sandra Webster: Desert Sands Necklace.

Chapter 4: Techniques for Wire Manipulation   42

Chapter 5: Off the Cuff – Wire Wrapped Cuffs   61

Chapter 6: Rings   70

Chapter 7: Coiling Gizmo Basics   78

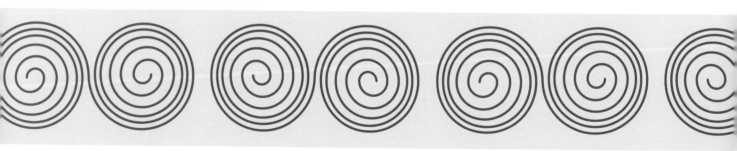

Courtesy of LeRoy Goertz: Coiling Gizmo.

Chapter 8: Coiling By Design   93

Chapter 9: Jump Rings And Assemblage   102

Glossary   111

Index   117

Contributors   124

About the Photographers: WILLIAM ALLEN, CAS WEBBER   124

About the Author: Susan Ray   125

Resource Guide   126

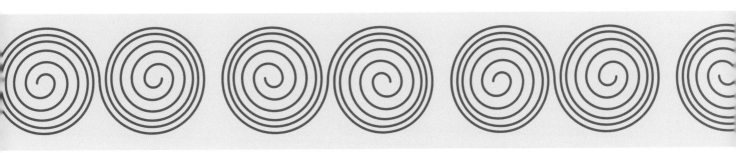

Courtesy of Gary Helwig, WigJig.

Kathleen Manning,
Courtesy of Beadazzled, Inc.

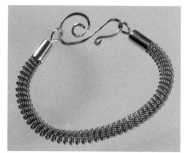

Courtesy of LeRoy Goertz,
Coiling Gizmo.

Introduction by Author Susan Ray

It was during the writing of *Beaded Jewelry: The Complete Guide* that *Wire Jewelry Workshop* was born. Handcrafted wire jewelry, prevalent around the world throughout history, was becoming popular at the boutiques once again. Designs change over time. Fads come and go. Everything is cycled. But today's new wire jewelry designs are so compelling; I had to write about them. The plain fact is that some of the most intriguing and beautiful jewelry today incorporates beads and wire.

In reviewing projects made with wire for this book, I was immediately taken with the ease at which you can add these exciting techniques into your own work. *Wire Jewelry Workshop* will give you a glimpse into the many techniques and tools used today. Many of these same designs are being sold by top designers selling to boutiques nationwide. And you can create them, teach them and sell them too!

To begin my journey, I went to the experts. Gary Helwig, creator of the Delphi and Centaur WigJigs, explained that "wire is relatively new, starting in Roman times about 2000 years ago." Today, we have many new tools to make the handwork easier than in those days. Gary adds: "In Roman times, wire was made from flat sheets of metal that were rolled between wooden blocks into small tubes of wire. Modern wire is made by pulling the metal through progressively smaller openings until you reach the size you need," creating many different gauges. And, Gary should know. He is the creator of the WigJig, a modern tool that is actually a block with a matrix of holes and pegs to fit into the holes. The jig is used to establish patterns, allowing you to create delicate loops for ear wires, chandelier earrings, connectors, bracelets, and necklace components. You will be amazed at the quality of the work, and hear from the founder himself how to best accomplish each technique. You will see how to use your own creativity to accomplish well-crafted, elegant jewelry components simply and easily.

And, when the bug bites, please visit Gary's Web site: www.wigjig.com for many more project ideas.

Gary also teaches you the correct techniques for cutting wire, straightening wire, bending wire, making a "P"-loop, making an eye loop, making a wrapped loop, opening and closing loops, and the basics for using a jewelry-making jig, one of the most commonly used tools in making jewelry with wire and beads. Gary is a master craftsman. He provides an unwavering commitment to present step by steps that are clear and concise. "Cutting wire may seem to be obvious, but it requires education and experience," says Gary. There is much to learn, all here in this volume, *Wire Jewelry Workshop: Techniques for Working With Wire and Beads*.

And this is just the beginning of the fun! You will also learn to make some sophisticated rings made by Ilene Baranowitz and Kathleen Manning. These sterling wire rings are easy and so much fun! I have also included the "Train Wreck" ring taught to me by a customer at my bead store years ago. This is a real crowd pleaser. You can introduce even the youngest bead enthusiast to beading by giving them some craft wire and beads; and, re-create this "train wreck" ring time and time again. The possibilities are endless, the supplies are inexpensive, and you will really love the results.

More possibilities for designing and making wire and beaded jewelry continue with LeRoy Goertz, another wire works expert. LeRoy is the creator of the Coiling Gizmo, a tool that makes, for one, handcrafted wire beads by coiling wire around a mandrel. Discover how to create a wrapped bead, a basic wire choker, or a wire-wrapped beaded clasp using this simple tool and easy instructions, again, directly from the expert. You will learn to coil simple yet unique looks to add to your beaded jewelry repertoire. LeRoy's vision and his new Deluxe Coiling Gizmo make the work of creating intricate, handmade wire designs so much fun.

Courtesy of Beadazzled, Tyson, Va. Photography by William L. Allen.

Jeanne Holland: The Briny Deep Choker. Courtesy of Vintaj Natural Brass Co.

Sandra Webster: Desert Rose Cuff Bracelet. Courtesy of Sandra Webster Jewelry.

If you're intrigued by the possibilities of designing and making wire jewelry, then you will enjoy the pages within. You will be given a front row seat at the work tables of many of the industry's top designers. Learn how to create an array of new fashion trends and the tricks of the trade from: Ilene Baranowitz, Sherrie Chapin, Leroy Goertz, Gary Helwig, Darien Kaiser, Jan Ketza Harris, Jeanne Holland, Jessica Italia, Trish Italia, Susan A. Karczewski, Deanna and Janet Killackey, Sue Kwong and Karen Li, Dotsie S. Mack, Kathleen Manning, Barbara Markoe, Mackenzie Mullane, Wendy Mullane, Cathie Roberts, Megan Starkey, Ronda Terry, Cas K. Webber, and Sandi Webster. You will find inspiration everywhere. Variety is the spice of life. The techniques and looks are diverse, so there will be something for every designer, from beginner to experienced and from young to those just "young at heart." These designers share with you their helpful hints and valuable techniques to create captivating jewelry for today's marketplace.

And please don't miss the artful Victorian-inspired work of Jeanne Holland from Vintaj Natural Brass Company in "Vintage Assemblage" or "Off the Cuff" with Sandi Webster, Cas K. Webber and Ronda Terry. Their cuff bracelets are filled with such creativity; and, Patrick Ober's Japanese 4-in-1 Chain Mail Bracelet is a distinctive look at a "chain" bracelet made entirely from jump rings.

Embrace your unique spirit. I hope this book will be the beginning of years of work with wire and beads. Please remember to share the wealth and pass along the techniques you learn. We all gain inspiration when we share.

Special wishes on your journey,

Susan Ray

Author's Note: Many of the designs in this book were prepared and photographed through the grace and generosity of Penelope Diamanti, William L. Allen and Cas K. Webber.

Adventures of a Lifetime — About Penelope Diamanti, owner of Beadazzled, Inc. in Virginia, Maryland, and Washington D.C.

The first traders Penelope met were Hausa vendor from Nigeria who presided over stalls in the Treichville Market in Abidjan, Ivory Coast, where she got hooked on beads. She visited the market almost daily, learning how to bargain — and about loyalties and economics. As tourists found their way into the market, Penelope saw them sometimes being charged high prices. She learned the traders felt the tourists had not earned the lower prices they offered to her, a "local" who bought from them every week in increasing quantities. By charging tourists more it enabled the traders to charge regulars, like her, less. This was her first lesson on wholesale versus retail.

It wasn't long before Penelope applied the lesson to herself when she became a bead trader. She returned to the U.S. with a tin safari trunk full of beads and began peddling them to fellow students, making and selling jewelry to friends, consigning to small boutiques, and vending at craft fairs and shows around the west.

As a passionate collector and designer, Penelope states that she couldn't have a better job than buying and selling beads. The opportunity to meet makers and users of beads in a variety of cultures on four continents has greatly increased her understanding of their production, history, and meaning. She'd committed to sharing what she has learned through the educational programs of her stores, her Web site (www.Beadazzled.net), her publications, including "Beadazzled, Where Beads and Inspiration Meet", and through her work with the Bead Society of Greater Washington and the Bead Museum. Her hope is to be able to continue to support and inspire designers, collectors, students of bead history, and entrepreneurs worldwide.

Wire by Hand

Midnight at the Oasis.
Courtesy of Cathie Roberts.

History of Wire With Gary Helwig

In the 10,000-year-plus history of making jewelry, wire is a relatively recent invention, dating back to the Roman times about 2,000 years ago. Many wire techniques have been improved by the introduction of tools that weren't available to the Romans.

In Roman times, wire was made from sheets of metal that were rolled between wooden blocks into small tubes. Sometimes these tubes were filled with sulfur to add strength to the wire. Modern wire is made by pulling metal through progressively smaller openings until the desired size is reached. Of these, 16 is the largest and most difficult to use. Eighteen- and 20-gauge wires are strong enough to make permanent wire components like the body of an earring or bracelet parts. Twenty-

Courtesy of Beadazzled. Photography by William L. Allen.

two and 24 gauges are very thin and are commonly used to make the links that connect wire components to one another. Outside of the U.S., many countries sell wire based on the size of the wire in millimeters (mm). Using this scale, 18-gauge wire is about 1 mm in diameter.

With precious metal wire (gold, gold-filled, and sterling silver) you can purchase wire with different hardness properties. The hardness of wire is a measure of how springy it is.

Dead-soft wire (hardness of 0) will not spring back. Soft wire is easy to push into shape as jewelry and easy to push out of shape. Hard wire (hardness of 4) will be very springy and hard to work with, but it is hard to push out of shape and therefore permanent. Half-hard wire (hardness of 2) is a compromise that is slightly springy, but firm enough that it will resist being pushed out of shape as a finished piece of jewelry.

Finally, wire can be hardened after it is purchased, both by working it (called work hardening) or by hammering it after it has been shaped.

In the United States, wire is measured using a scale called the American Wire Gauge, or simply, gauge. In this scale, a smaller number for the gauge means that the diameter of the wire is larger. Zero gauge wire is approximately the thickness of a pencil. For making jewelry with beads, 16-, 18-, 20-, 22- and 24-gauge wires are most commonly used.

Tools for Working With Wire

Courtesy of Gary Helwig, WigJig.

ROUND-NOSE PLIERS

Round-nose pliers have two conical jaws and are used for making loops in wire.

Rosary pliers also are used by some artists. These combine a round nose and a side cutter.

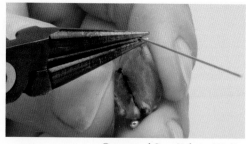

Courtesy of Gary Helwig, WigJig.

CHAIN-NOSE PLIERS

Chain-nose pliers have jaws that narrow at the tip and have a flat smooth inner surface. Chain-nose pliers are used for gripping and holding wire and for bending wire.

BENT CHAIN-NOSE PLIERS

Bent chain-nose pliers are preferred over chain-nose pliers with straight jaws. The bend allows you to work comfortably over a long period of time because your wrist remains straight.

Courtesy of Gary Helwig, WigJig.

FLUSH CUTTER

A flush cutter is a jewelry wire cutter that has one flat smooth side with the opposite side beveled to create a sharp edge. *Note: Wire cutters used by electricians will not work because they are beveled on both sides of the cutter, creating a sharp end on both sides of the cut wire.*

Courtesy of Gary Helwig, WigJig.

JAW PLIERS

Nylon-jaw pliers have jaws covered in nylon so that they do not scratch the wire. Nylon-jaw pliers are used for straightening wire and for flattening a finished wire component.

Step-jaw pliers have one jaw that is flat and smooth and the opposite jaw has three cylindrical steps increasing in size, from the smallest cylinder at the tip to the largest cylinder at the base of the jaws. Step-jaw pliers are used for making loops that are always the same diameter. The flat jaw of the step-jaw pliers will not mark your wire. Fewer marks on your wire and consistent size make these pliers useful for the initial loop in a wire component.

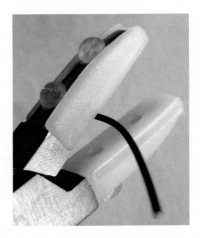

Courtesy of Gary Helwig, WigJig.

Courtesy of Gary Helwig, WigJig.

WIRE GAUGE CHART

Wire Width	Gauge	Diameter
—————.	28 gauge	.30 mm
—————.	26 gauge	.40 mm
—————.	24 gauge	.50 mm
—————.	22 gauge	.64 mm
—————.	20 gauge	.75 mm
—————•	18 gauge	1.00 mm
—————•	16 gauge	1.25 mm
—————•	14 gauge	1.50 mm
—————•	12 gauge	2.00 mm

CUP BUR

A cup bur is a special file used for rounding the end of jewelry wire. The cup bur has a tiny cup on the end with a filing surface inside the cup. This surface acts like sandpaper and leaves a rounded end on cut wire.

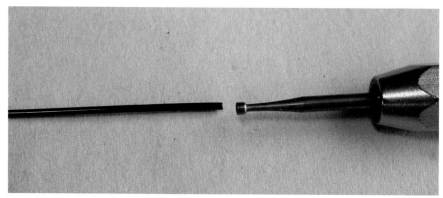

Courtesy of Gary Helwig, WigJig.

JIGS

A jig is a block with a matrix of holes and metal pegs to fit into the holes. The jig is used to establish patterns for making wire components. The jigs used in the projects below are the WigJig Centaur or the WigJig Delphi. These jigs have 1/16" metal pegs and a hole spacing of about five holes per inch on the horizontal axis. The size of the pegs used and the hole spacing are important, as this combination allows us to make smaller and more delicate wire components. The hole spacing on the diagonal axis is almost six holes per inch, which allows us to make even smaller wire components using the diagonal axis or larger wire components using the horizontal axis and vertical axis. These are features that we commonly use to make a larger component for a bracelet and a smaller component for an earring.

Courtesy of Gary Helwig, WigJig.

The WigJig tools were chosen for these projects because they are the only commercially available jigs that have smaller pegs and a more delicate peg pattern to use in these projects.

WIGJIG CENTAUR

The WigJig Centaur has a combination of the square peg pattern of the WigJig Delphi and half of the round peg pattern of the WigJig Cyclops combined in one jig, making the Centaur perhaps the most versatile jig on the market. You can also use the round pattern of the WigJig Centaur to make a wire component that expands away from the top of the piece at an angle of 30 degrees. This angle allows a necklace to naturally drape in a semi-circle similar to a human neck. (This is an important feature for a necklace — don't you agree?) For the earring and bracelet patterns that follow, the square pattern from the WigJig Delphi or the square portion of the WigJig Centaur were used.

Courtesy of Gary Helwig, WigJig.

Courtesy of Gary Helwig, WigJig.

   ▲

ROUND *HALF-ROUND* *SQUARE* *TRIANGLE* *TWIST*

Various wire shapes.

CHAPTER 2

Creating Wire Components

Wire Cutting Techniques

Courtesy of Gary Helwig, WigJig.

Flush   *Sharp*

Cutting wire may seem to be obvious, but it requires education and experience. Jewelry wire cutters, called flush cutters, are made to cut wire leaving one side flush or flat and the opposite side sharp or pointed. The cutters have one flat side and one beveled side. The wire cut on the flat side of the cutter will be left with a flush or flat end. The wire cut on the beveled side of the cutter will be left with a sharp or pointed end. The important thing in making jewelry is that the wire in your finished jewelry must have the flat or flush ends instead of sharp ends. By orienting the flat jaw of your flush cutter toward your finished piece, this can be easily accomplished.

Making a "P" Loop

A basic skill is making a simple loop called a "P" loop. This loop is named for its resemblance to the letter P.

STEP A: Using a round-nose pliers, grasp the end of your wire with the flush cut in the jaws of your pliers. Try to grip the wire with a minimum of excess wire beyond the jaws of your pliers. This takes a little practice.

Courtesy of Gary Helwig, WigJig.

STEP B: Holding your pliers in your non-dominant hand, push the wire with the thumb of your dominant hand up, over and around the jaws of your pliers. Push with your thumb as close to the jaws of the pliers as possible.

STEP C: This will leave you with a "P" loop in the end of your wire.

Courtesy of Gary Helwig, WigJig.

Straightening Wire

This skill is important to every jewelry project that starts with straightening the wire. Wire is delivered with a natural curl, which you must remove before shaping the wire for jewelry. Cut the wire to length, then make a loop in the end of the wire. Straighten the wire by holding the loop and pulling the wire repeatedly through the nylon jaw pliers. Hold and squeeze the nylon jaw pliers in your non-dominant hand, and grip and pull the loop in the end of the wire, using your thumb and forefinger on your dominant hand.

For every jewelry project, start with straight wire and stop and straighten your wire if it accidentally becomes bent.

Courtesy of Gary Helwig, WigJig.

Bending Wire

Many jewelry techniques require us to make a bend of about 90 degrees in the wire.

STEP A: Grasp and hold the wire using the bent chain-nose pliers, positioning the wire in the jaws of your pliers at the point where the bend is needed.

STEP B: While holding the pliers with your non-dominant hand, use the thumb of your dominant hand and push the wire with your thumb as close to the jaws of the pliers as possible. Your goal is a crisp, sharp angle.

Courtesy of Gary Helwig, WigJig.

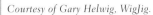

Courtesy of Gary Helwig, WigJig.

Making an Eye Loop

For some wire jewelry components, the simple "P" loop is not appropriate, so you will need to make an eye loop. An eye loop is a round loop centered on the wire stem like a lollipop.

STEP A: Start with a segment of straight wire at least 3" long. Half-hard wire is preferred, but soft wire will work.

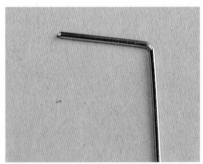

Courtesy of Gary Helwig, WigJig.

STEP B: Using bent chain-nose pliers, bend the wire at a 90-degree angle about ½" to ¾" from the end of the wire.

Courtesy of Gary Helwig, WigJig.

STEP C: Using round-nose pliers, grasp the wire on the short, horizontal segment, as close to the bend as possible.

STEP D: While holding the round-nose pliers in your non-dominant hand, use the thumb of your dominant hand to push the wire up and over the jaw of the round-nose pliers. At this point the wire will look like an upside down "U."

Courtesy of Gary Helwig, WigJig.

STEP E: To turn this "U" into an eye loop, re-grip the wire component in the jaws of the pliers. Re-orient the wire on the pliers so when the jaws of the pliers are horizontal, the wire is also horizontal, pointing away from the pliers.

STEP F: Push the wire tail down to complete a loop around the jaw of the pliers.

STEP G: Visually inspect the loop, and while still gripping the loop in the pliers, adjust the loop so that the wire stem is centered on the loop.

STEP H: Remove the wire from your pliers. You are ready to cut the excess wire. Position the flush cutter at the point where the wire tail crosses the stem. Remember that the flat side of the cutter should be on the side of the finished loop.

Courtesy of Gary Helwig, WigJig.

STEP I: After cutting the wire, the loop will be slightly open. To close, grasp the wire with bent chain-nose pliers and twist the wire to close the loop.

Courtesy of Gary Helwig, WigJig.

L173, 467/745.5942

Making an Eyepin Pendant Bail

MacKenzie Mullane: Bona Fide Beachcomber Bracelet.

GATHERING YOUR GOODS

- 1 sterling silver ¾" turtle bead
- 1 natural brass 1½" eyepin

TOOLS TO HAVE ON HAND

- Chain-nose pliers (2 pairs)
- Rosary pliers with side cutter

Designer: **Mackenzie Mullane**
Expense: **$25 to $50**
Expertise: **Intermediate**

MAKING THE EYEPIN BAIL

STEP A: Bend the eyepin into a "U" shape. The loop should be approximately ¼" above the bead. The pendant non-looped end will be approximately ½" above the bead pendant.

STEP B: Coil the non-looped end of the eyepin around the looped end of the eyepin. Gently tighten and straighten using chain-nose pliers. Your pendant is complete.

STRINGING THE BEAD ONTO THE EYEPIN

Hold the turtle bead facing toward you on its side. Slide the eyepin through the hole in the bead.

Opening and Closing Jump Rings

Open jump ring.

Frequently, jewelry components connect parts using loops. The loop may be part of the component or it may be a connector like a jump ring finding that you purchase, or a figure-eight connector that you make. Open or close loops or jump rings by grasping one side of the loop with bent chain-nose pliers and twisting side to side.

    To close a loop, twist the pliers clockwise back in place. For some people this approach is counterintuitive. It might seem that you would want to pull down on the pliers. Unfortunately, pulling the loop apart distorts the loop permanently.

Techniques for Using a Jig

There are many jigs for making jewelry on the market now, and, as with all tools, there are right ways and wrong ways to use them. Here are a few suggestions that will make using a jig easier.

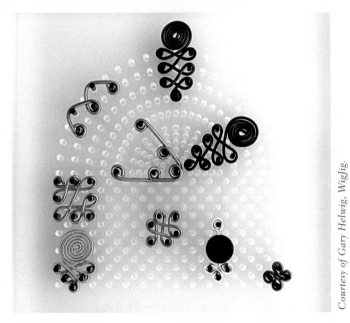

Courtesy of Gary Helwig, Wiglig.

STEP A: When using a jig, start all patterns by fixing the wire to the jig, using a loop in the wire over a peg in the jig. This applies to all patterns — even those patterns where you will be cutting off the loop after the wire component is completed.

STEP B: Most patterns will work better by starting with only two pegs in the jig. Place the initial loop on the first peg and bend the wire against the second peg, per your pattern.

STEP C: Continue to wrap your wire, adding a peg as you go. If you begin with a pattern of 10 pegs, and all 10 pegs are in your jig, eight of them will be in your way. Simply stated, start with two pegs and add as you go.

STEP D: Wire is naturally springy, especially half-hard wire. If you push it 30 degrees and then let go, the wire may spring back 10 degrees. When making a wire component on a jig, push the wire beyond where you want the wire to stay, and remove the grip on the wire to see where it will stay. Making a wire component on a jig is a series of pushing the wire, removing the grip to see if the wire stays where you want it, and then pushing more if necessary.

STEP E: Push the wire with your fingers as close to the pegs on the jig as possible. The operative word here is "push." You will not be successful if you grab the wire by its end and try to pull the wire into position. This will introduce unwanted bends in your wire.

STEP F: When making a wire component on a jig, always start with straight wire and keep the unused wire straight as you go. In general, the easiest way to keep your wire straight is to hold the wire and push the wire with your dominant hand, while you turn the jig in your non-dominant hand.

STEP G: A good jewelry-making practice is to make any new jewelry item three times using inexpensive practice wire that you plan to throw away, before making a finished piece using good wire. Measure the amount of wire you used on these practice pieces, so that when you are ready to use your expensive wire, you can cut the correct amount.

Courtesy of Gary Helwig, WigJig.

GATHERING
YOUR GOODS

12	Swarovski 6 mm crystal beads or crystal pearls
4	metal 2.5 mm round beads
15"	wire, 16-gauge, 18-gauge, or 20-gauge
30"	wire, 20-gauge, 21-gauge or 22-gauge
	Clasp finding
3"	fine commercial chain for guard chain (optional)

3:2:1 WigJig
Bracelet

TOOLS
TO HAVE ON HAND

- Flush cutter
- Round-nose pliers
- Bent chain-nose pliers (2)
- Nylon-jaw pliers
- WigJig Centaur or WigJig Delphi jig
- Fine step-jaw pliers (optional)

Designer: Gary Helwig
Finished Size: 7½" long by 1¼" wide

Expense: Under $25
Expertise: Intermediate
Time to Complete: An evening

This project is called the 3:2:1 WigJig Bracelet for a simple reason. It is made of three wire components, each one made on a jig. The central wire component has three loops on each side. On either side of this central wire component are wire components that have two loops on each side. On either side of these components is our final pair of wire components, each having two loops on one side and one loop on the other. For simplicity, we will call these wire components the 3-loop wire component, the 2-loop wire component and the 2:1 wire component.

Making this bracelet is accomplished with four techniques — one technique for making each of the three-wire components, plus a technique to connect the wire components into a finished bracelet.

MAKING THE 3-LOOP WIRE COMPONENT

STEP A: Cut a wire segment of 16-, 18-, or 20-gauge wire 5¼" long. Half-hard wire is preferred, but soft wire will also work.

STEP B: Using the end of the wire with the flush cut, make a loop in one end of this wire segment with your round-nose pliers or step-jaw pliers, if you have them.

Courtesy of Gary Helwig, WigJig

STEP C: Straighten the wire segment by pulling it through the jaws of your nylon-jaw pliers.

STEP D: Position pegs 1 and 2 in your jig, and place the initial loop in your wire segment on peg 1.

STEP E: Applying pressure, wrap the wire around peg 2, leaving the wire adjacent to the empty hole for peg 3.

STEP F: Add peg 3 to your pattern. Without applying pressure, wrap the wire around peg 3, so that it rests adjacent to the empty hole for peg 4.

STEP G: Add peg 4 to your pattern. Without applying pressure, wrap the wire around peg 4, so that it rests adjacent to the empty hole for peg 5.

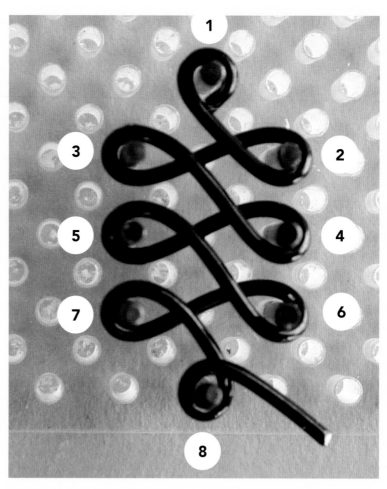

Courtesy of Gary Helwig, WigJig

STEP H: Add peg 5 to your pattern. Without applying pressure, wrap the wire around peg 5 so that it rests adjacent to the empty hole for peg 6.

STEP I: Add peg 6 to your pattern. Without applying pressure, wrap the wire around peg 6, so that it rests adjacent to the empty hole for peg 7.

STEP J: Add peg 7 to your pattern. Without applying pressure, wrap the wire around peg 7, so that it rests adjacent to the empty hole for peg 8.

STEP K: Add peg 8 to your pattern. Wrap the wire tightly around this peg.

STEP L: Remove the wire from your jig and cut the excess wire. Remember to properly orient your flush cutter.

STEP M: Using your bent chain-nose pliers, close the loop made on peg 8.

STEP N: Using your nylon-jaw pliers, squeeze the wire component in several orientations to flatten and harden the piece. Hand-finish the piece.

Note: Hand-finishing a piece is the process of bending the wire gently with your fingers so that it is as symmetrical as possible.

MAKING THE 2-LOOP WIRE COMPONENTS

STEP A: Cut a wire segment of 16-, 18-, or 20-gauge wire 4" long. Half-hard wire is preferred, but soft wire will also work.

STEP B: Make a loop in the end of this wire segment with your round-nose pliers or step-jaw pliers, if you have them.

STEP C: Straighten this wire segment by pulling it through the jaws of your nylon-jaw pliers.

STEP D: Position pegs 9 and 10 in your jig and place your initial loop in your wire segment on peg 9.

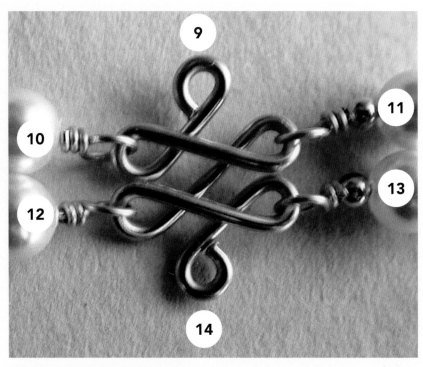

WigJig Centaur. Courtesy of Gary Helwig, WigJig.

STEP E: Without applying pressure, wrap the wire around peg 10, leaving the wire adjacent to the empty hole for peg 11.

STEP F: Add peg 11 to your pattern. Without applying pressure, wrap the wire around peg 11 so that it rests adjacent to the hole for peg 12.

STEP G: Add peg 12 to your pattern. Without applying pressure, wrap the wire around peg 12 so that it rests adjacent to the hole for peg 13.

STEP H: Add peg 13 to your pattern. Without applying pressure, wrap the wire around peg 13 so that it rests adjacent to the hole for peg 14.

STEP I: Add peg 14 to your pattern and wrap the wire tightly around peg 14.

STEP J: Remove the wire from your jig and cut the excess wire. Remember to orient the flat side of your flush cutter toward the finished piece.

STEP K: Using your bent chain-nose pliers, close the loop made on peg 14.

STEP L: Using your nylon-jaw pliers, squeeze the wire component in several orientations to flatten and harden the piece. Hand-finish the piece by bending the wire gently with your fingers, so that it is as symmetrical as possible.

STEP M: Make two of these wire components.

Courtesy of Gary Helwig, WigJig.

MAKING THE 2:1 WIRE COMPONENTS

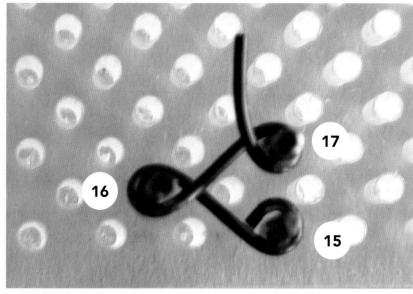

Courtesy of Gary Helwig, WigJig.

STEP A: Cut a wire segment of 16-, 18-, or 20-gauge round wire 2" long. Half-hard wire is preferred, but soft wire will also work.

STEP B: Make a loop in the end of this wire segment with your round-nose pliers or step-jaw pliers, if you have them.

STEP C: Straighten this wire segment by pulling it through the jaws of your nylon-jaw pliers.

STEP D: Position pegs 15 and 16 in your jig. Place your initial loop on peg 15, oriented as indicated.

STEP E: Without applying pressure, wrap the wire around peg 16, so that the wire rests against the empty hole for peg 17.

STEP F: Add peg 17 to your pattern. Wrap your wire tightly around the peg.

STEP G: Remove the wire from your jig and cut the excess wire with the flat side of your flush cutter toward the finished piece.

STEP H: Using your bent chain-nose pliers, close the loop made on peg 17.

STEP I: Using your nylon-jaw pliers, squeeze the wire component in several orientations to flatten and harden the piece. Hand-finish the piece to make it symmetrical.

STEP J: Make two of these wire components.

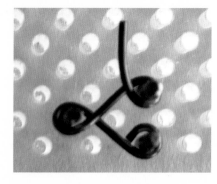

Courtesy of Gary Helwig, WigJig.

While you are learning to make this piece, start with 20-gauge practice wire and graduate to 18 for your first finished bracelet. The finished bracelet will look better made in 16-gauge wire, but it will be easier to learn to make this piece in 20-gauge and then 18-gauge wire. For directions on how to make loops in 16-gauge wire, please visit the following web page: http://www.wigjig.com/jewelry-making/loops/pg05.htm.

Using good wire (half-hard wire), will help to make these wire components more consistent when you are ready to make your finished bracelet.

Wrapped Bead Links

To connect the wire components, you can use the wrapped bead link. Each wire component is connected to the components on either side with two wrapped bead links. Make the first of these two links. Follow directions for the wrapped bead technique. (See page 28.) Making the second of these two wrapped bead links is slightly more difficult because the first wrapped bead link will be in your way. Again, follow the regular steps for making a wrapped bead link, including connecting the initial wrapped loop into its position on one of the wire components and adding the bead. Bend the wire over to 90 degrees. Make the second loop in the wire with your round-nose pliers pointing toward the outside, away from the first wrapped bead loop. Wrap so that the unused wire tail is on the outside, away from the center. In the orientation shown, the pliers will be pointing toward the bottom of the picture to make the second loop. Cut the excess wire to a length of only ½".

Connect that second loop into its position. You should have enough room to grasp and hold that loop with your bent chain-nose pliers while you wrap that loop closed.

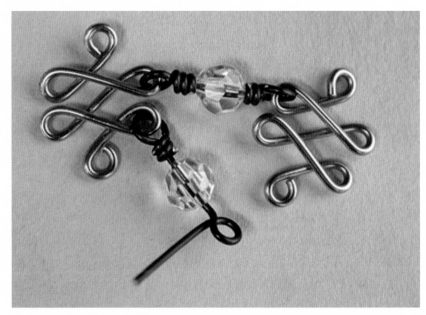

Courtesy of Gary Helwig, WigJig.

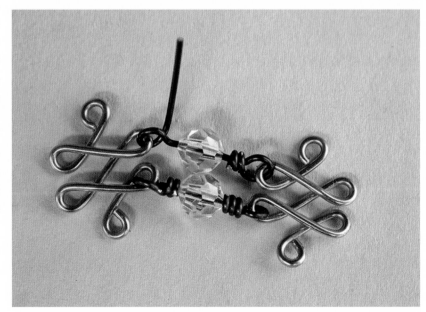

Courtesy of Gary Helwig, WigJig.

CONNECTING THE COMPONENTS

STEP A: We begin making this bracelet from the center. Make a wrapped bead link to connect the top left loop on the 3-loop wire component to the top right loop on one of the 2-loop wire components. Use the largest wire that will fit through your beads (20-, 21- or 22-gauge half-hard wire is preferred). Use a 6 mm bead and two 2.5 mm round metal beads for the wrapped bead link. (The 2.5 mm metal beads are optional. The added space they provide will make it easier to make the two wrapped bead links.) When the first wrapped bead link is completed, connect the bottom left loop on your 3-loop wire component to the bottom right loop on the 2-loop wire component.

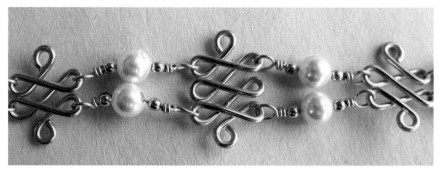

Courtesy of Gary Helwig, WigJig.

Courtesy of Gary Helwig, WigJig.

STEP B: Connect the 2-loop wire component to the opposite side of the 3-loop wire component, using the same approach described above.

STEP C: Connect the left 2-loop wire component to the left 2:1 wire component. First, connect the top loops, using a wrapped bead link, then connect the bottom loops. For these two wrapped bead links, only a single 6 mm bead was used. (The 2.5 mm metal beads can be used, if you like that look.)

STEP D: Connect the right side 2-loop wire component to the right 2:1 wire component using two wrapped bead links, each with a 6 mm bead.

STEP E: Finish the bracelet. Use two wrapped bead links to connect the single loop in the 2:1 wire connector to the clasp on each side. Add these two wrapped bead links to both sides of the bracelet, and connect the clasp on either end. Use 6 mm beads for each of the wrapped bead links.

STEP F: If you are using a magnetic clasp or another clasp that isn't totally secure, add a guard chain to the bracelet using about 3" of fine commercial chain. You can connect the guard chain after the clasp has been completed using either a jump-ring finding or a figure-eight connector. A better way is to connect the guard chain to the wrapped bead link at the same time that you add the clasp. When the loop in the wrapped bead link is wrapped closed, the guard chain is permanently connected. With a magnetic clasp, a guard chain is mandatory for a bracelet. For other types of clasps, it is optional.

Courtesy of Gary Helwig, WigJig.

CHAPTER 3

Dangles: Wrapped Wire Method

A

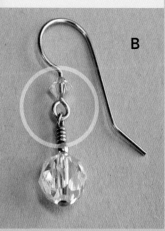

B

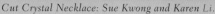

Cut Crystal Necklace: Sue Kwong and Karen Li.

A bead dangle is a decorative way of hanging a bead from a loop. A bead dangle can be made with an open loop or with a wrapped loop. We will discuss both techniques in this chapter. Both techniques begin using an approach similar to the technique used to make an eye loop, with slight modifications.

You can see both types of completed bead dangles here. The top is the bead dangle with the eye loop (A); the bottom is the bead dangle with the wrapped loop (B).

Making a Wrapped Bead Link

Wrapped bead links are strong and are frequently used in making bracelets, necklaces and rosaries. You can also use this approach when making chandelier earrings. The wrapped bead link technique is basically used to connect a loop on one wire component to a loop on another wire component using wire and a bead.

Courtesy of Gary Helwig, WigJig.

STEP A: Begin with a segment of 20-, 22-, or 24-gauge round wire at least 3" long. Half-hard wire will work better, if it is available. Use the largest gauge of wire that will comfortably fit through the beads you intend to use. (Glass beads can saw through thin wire. This usually happens only in bracelets because they experience a lot of motion when worn. This won't happen overnight, but in time with normal wear, you may find your beads cutting through thinner wire.)

STEP B: Grasp the wire about 1" from the end with the bent chain-nose pliers and make a bend of about 90 degrees.

Courtesy of Gary Helwig, WigJig.

STEP C: Using the round-nose pliers, grip the wire on the shorter, 1" segment, but as close to the 90-degree bend as possible.

Courtesy of Gary Helwig, WigJig.

28

STEP D: Using the thumb of your dominant hand, push the wire up and over the jaw of the pliers. Try to push the wire with your thumb as close to the pliers as possible.

STEP E: Reposition the wire so that you can complete a loop in the wire. With the jaws of the pliers horizontal (your wire should also be horizontal), pointing away from the pliers, begin the loop.

STEP F: Push the wire to complete a full loop.

STEP G: Before removing the wire from the pliers, adjust the long wire tail so that it is centered on the loop in the pliers. This may require pushing the wire tail left or right until it is centered.

STEP H: Remove the wire from the pliers and connect this loop to the prior loop in the project. This could be a loop in a wire component that you made, it could be the loop in a clasp, or it could be a similar wrapped bead link that you made.

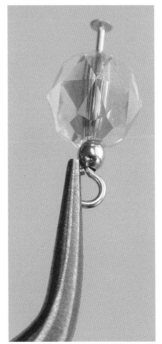

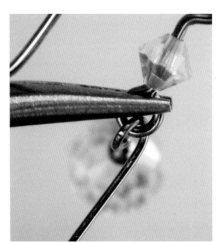

Courtesy of Gary Helwig, WigJig.

Courtesy of Gary Helwig, WigJig.

Courtesy of Gary Helwig, WigJig.

STEP I: Grasp the partially completed loop with the bent chain-nose pliers, and, while holding this loop firmly, wrap the short wire segment around the longer wire segment about two and one-half times.

STEP J: Using your flush cutter, cut the excess wire, remembering to properly orient the flush cutter.

STEP K: Now, you'll need to squeeze and twist the cut end so that it won't stick up. Grasp the loop in the wire with the bent chain-nose pliers and with a second pair of chain-nose pliers, squeeze and twist the cut end of the wire until it lies flat.

STEP L: At this point you are ready to add one or more beads.

STEP M: Slide the beads all the way down and using the bent chain-nose pliers, grip the wire immediately above the beads.

STEP N: Bend the wire over to about 90 degrees. Where you grip the wire on the bent chain-nose pliers and the thickness of the pliers will determine the distance between the bead and the 90-degree bend. If possible, grip the wire so that this distance is always ⅛".

STEP O: At this point, we begin the process of making a wrapped loop again. Grip the wire as close to the 90-degree bend as possible with your round-nose pliers.

STEP P: Continue making the wrapped loop by pushing the wire up and over the jaw of your pliers, following steps D through K. When you are done, you will have connected two wire components using the wrapped bead link.

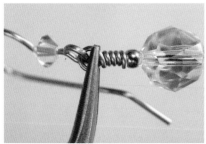

Courtesy of Gary Helwig, WigJig.

Courtesy of Gary Helwig, WigJig.

Making an Ear Wire Finding

Why would you make an ear wire when you can buy a machine-made ear wire at a reasonable price? There are two answers to this question. First, it makes sense to make an ear wire only if you are making some-thing different than the machine makes. In the ear wire pictured, we included a 4 mm amethyst bead and plan to use this ear wire to make an earring containing amethyst beads. This technique makes the ear wire stand out as something that wasn't made by a machine and it adds value to the finished earrings. Another reason for making ear wires — sometimes you just run out and don't have any machine-made earrings available.

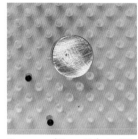

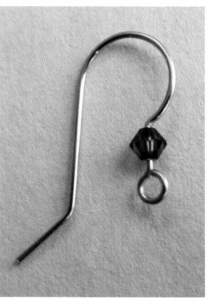

Courtesy of Gary Helwig, WigJig.

Courtesy of Gary Helwig, WigJig.

STEP A: Cut a 3" segment of 20-gauge round wire. Half-hard wire is preferred.

STEP B: Straighten this wire using nylon-jaw pliers.

STEP C: Make an eye loop in the end of this wire using the techniques described on page 19.

Courtesy of Gary Helwig, WigJig.

STEP D: Slide a 4 mm bead onto your wire. Slide the bead down so that it rests against the eye loop.

STEP E: Grip the wire immediately above the bead with your bent chain-nose pliers. Use the tips of your pliers so the thickness of the wire above the bead is minimized.

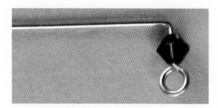

Courtesy of Gary Helwig, WigJig.

STEP F: Bend the wire over to an angle of about 80 degrees.

Courtesy of Gary Helwig, WigJig.

STEP G: The peg pattern for making this ear wire on a jig uses two metal pegs and a ⁵⁄₁₆" Super Peg. This pattern is shown below on the WigJig Centaur. Begin making this ear wire on the jig using peg 1 and 2 (remove peg 3). Place the eye loop in your wire on peg 1 as shown.

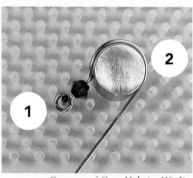

Courtesy of Gary Helwig, WigJig.

STEP H: Wrap the wire around peg 2 so that it rests adjacent to the hole for peg 3, without applying pressure.

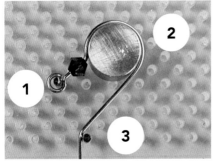

STEP I: Add peg 3 to the pattern and bend the wire against peg 3 to an angle of about 30 degrees.

STEP J: Remove the ear wire from the jig and cut the wire about ¼" from the bend at peg 3. Remember to cut the wire with the flat side of your flush cutter toward the finished ear wire. This is extremely important here because a sharp end on the wire is not acceptable.

STEP K: Using a file, like a nail file, or a cup bur tool, file the ends of the cut wire to round the end.

STEP L: If you have a nylon hammer or chasing hammer and anvil or a jeweler's block, hammer the rounded portion of the ear wire. This is the portion of the wire that touched the Super Peg. Using a nylon or rawhide hammer will harden the rounded portion of the ear wire without changing the round shape of the wire. Using a chasing hammer will flatten the wire where you hammer and will harden the finished ear wire more than the nylon hammer would. (Please note that most machine-made ear wires have the rounded portion of the ear wire flattened.)

Your finished ear wire will perfectly complement any earrings with matching beads.

More Earring Shapes

Balanced Squares Earrings: Susan Ray.

Labyrinths Earrings: Susan Ray.

Sugar Plum Swirls Earrings: Darien Kaiser.

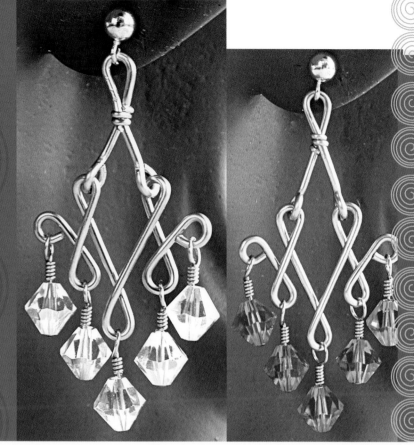

Courtesy of Gary Helwig, WigJig.

GATHERING YOUR GOODS

10	Swarovski 6 mm crystal beads or crystal pearls
15"	18-gauge or 20-gauge wire
4"	21-gauge half-round or 22- or 24-gauge round wire
10	headpin findings, 1½"
1 pair	ear wire findings

TOOLS TO HAVE ON HAND

- Flush cutter
- Round-nose pliers
- Bent chain-nose pliers (2)
- Nylon-jaw pliers
- WigJig Centaur or WigJig Delphi jig
- Fine step-jaw pliers (optional)

Designer: Gary Helwig
Finished Size: 1¾" tall by ¾" wide
Expense: Under $25
Expertise: Intermediate
Time to Complete: An evening

Susan's Chandelier
Earrings

There are many ways to make wire components for earrings. Some are easy and elegant and others are more difficult. This earring design is based on a concept that can be easily adapted to many different earring designs. The concept is simple and elegant. The earrings are made of two wire components that are connected to one another using eye loops that are rotated 90 degrees. For simplicity, we will call these two

wire components the top wire component and the earring body. The top wire component looks somewhat like an inverted letter "Y." Essentially, it has one loop on top for connecting to the ear wire and two eye loops on the bottom, which are rotated 90 degrees so that they can connect to the earring body. We can use any style of earring body as long as the piece has two symmetrical loops that we can connect to the top wire component. The

power in this concept for making earrings is that using the two connected wire components like these will allow us to easily make many different earring designs in a variety of shapes. For this particular earring, we will use an earring body that is similar in construction to the wire components that we will make later for our bracelet and necklace projects.

MAKING THE EARRING BODY

Courtesy of Gary Helwig, WigJig.

STEP A: Cut a 4¾" segment of 18- or 20-gauge round wire. (Half-hard wire will work better than soft.)

STEP B: Using your round-nose pliers, make a "P" loop in the end of the wire segment, sized to fit over one of the pegs on your jig. (See the instructions for making a "P" loop, page 18.) When making your "P" loop, start with the flush cut end of your wire segment.

STEP C: Using your nylon-jaw pliers, straighten the wire segment.

STEP E: Add peg 3 to your pattern. Without applying pressure, wrap the wire around peg 3 so that the wire rests adjacent to the hole for peg 4.

STEP F: Add peg 4 to your pattern. Without applying pressure, wrap the wire around peg 4 so that wire rests adjacent to the hole for peg 5.

STEP G: Add peg 5 to your pattern. Without applying pressure, wrap the wire around peg 5 so that the wire rests adjacent to the hole for peg 6.

STEP H: Add peg 6 to your pattern. Without applying pressure, wrap the wire around peg 6 so that the wire rests adjacent to the hole for peg 7.

STEP I: Add peg 7. Wrap the wire around peg 7.

STEP J: Remove your wire component from the jig. Using your flush cutter, cut the excess wire with the flat side of your cutter toward the finished piece.

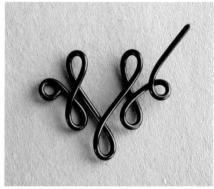

Courtesy of Gary Helwig, WigJig.

STEP K: Using your bent chain-nose pliers, close the loop in the wire component made on peg 7.

STEP L: Using your nylon-jaw pliers, squeeze the wire component in different orientations to flatten the piece and set the design. Using your fingers, hand-finish the piece so that it is as symmetrical as possible.

STEP M: Set this component aside; this is your earring body.

STEP D: The pattern for making the earring body on a jig appears as shown on the right. This pattern uses seven metal pegs, but as we do with all patterns made on a jig, we begin by putting only two pegs into our jig. Position pegs 1 and 2 in your jig. Place your initial loop for your wire segment on peg 1, oriented as shown, and wrap the wire around peg 2 so that with no pressure applied, the wire will rest adjacent to the empty hole for peg 3.

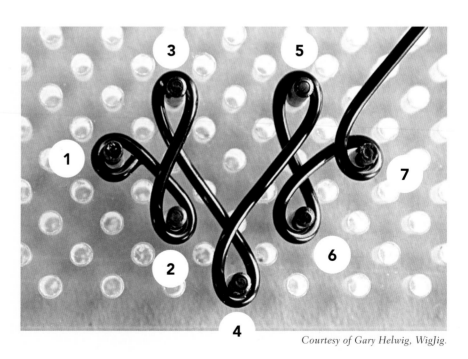

Courtesy of Gary Helwig, WigJig.

MAKING THE TOP WIRE COMPONENT

STEP A: Using your flush cutter, cut a 2¼" segment of 18- or 20-gauge wire. (If available, half-hard wire will work more consistently for this piece.)

STEP B: Using the end of the wire with the flush cut, take your round-nose pliers and make a "P" loop in one end of the wire.

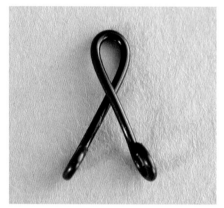

Courtesy of Gary Helwig, WigJig.

STEP C: Using your nylon-jaw pliers, straighten the wire.

STEP D: Position pegs 8 and 9 in your jig as shown below. Place your initial loop on peg 8. Without applying pressure, wrap the wire around peg 9 so that the wire rests adjacent to the empty hole for peg 10.

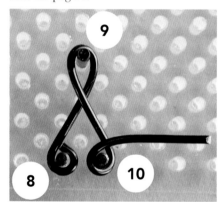

Courtesy of Gary Helwig, WigJig.

STEP E: Add peg 10 to your jig. Wrap your wire around peg 10.

STEP F: Remove the wire from your jig. Using your flush cutter, cut the excess wire with the flat side of your cutter toward the finished piece.

Courtesy of Gary Helwig, WigJig.

STEP G: Using your bent chain-nose pliers, close the loop made on peg 10.

Courtesy of Gary Helwig, WigJig.

STEP H: Using the tips of your round-nose pliers, twist the loops made on pegs 8 and 10 so that they become eye loops. (This is an alternate approach for making an eye loop.) In the picture shown, the pliers would be twisted in a clockwise direction from the perspective of the camera. For the opposite loop, you would need to twist your pliers counter-clockwise.

Courtesy of Gary Helwig, WigJig.

STEP I: Hold the loop made around peg 9 with your thumb and index finger using your non-dominant hand, and grip the loop made on peg 8 with your bent chain-nose pliers. Rotate that loop 90 degrees. See Step J for what the top wire component will look like after twisting the loop.

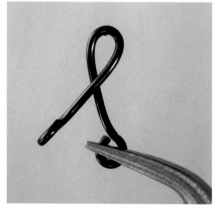

Courtesy of Gary Helwig, WigJig.

STEP J: Hold the loop made around peg 9 with the thumb and index finger of your non-dominant hand, and grip the loop made on peg 10 with your bent chain-nose pliers and rotate 90 degrees. If you rotated clockwise in Step I, you need to rotate counter-clockwise here, so that the open side of both loops is on the same side of the top wire component. Inspect this piece. Using your fingers or pliers, make the piece as symmetrical as possible. This is your finished top wire component.

ASSEMBLING THE WIRE COMPONENTS

STEP A: First, we need to connect the top wire component to the earring body. Using your bent chain-nose pliers, open the loops made in the top wire component on pegs 8 and 10. Connect these open loops to the loops made on your earring body on pegs 3 and 5. Once they are connected, use your bent chain-nose pliers to close both open loops.

Courtesy of Gary Helwig, WigJig.

STEP B: Once the wire components are connected, we are ready to use fine-gauge wire to wrap around the neck of the top wire component. Cut a 2" segment of fine-gauge wire. (Half-round, half-hard wire will work better, if available. If you don't have any half-round wire, use 22- or 24-gauge round wire.)

STEP C: Using the tips of the jaws of your round-nose pliers, make the smallest "U"-shaped bend that you can, about ½" from one end of the wire.

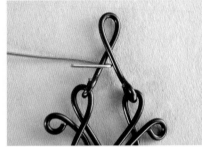

Courtesy of Gary Helwig, WigJig.

STEP D: Position the bottom of the "U" around one of the wire segments near the neck of the top wire component. Hold the short leg of the "U" with your thumb and forefinger of your non-dominant hand. Use the thumb of your dominant hand to push the longer leg of the "U" so that it wraps around the neck of the top wire component two or three times.

STEP E: Cut the excess wire so the ends of the wire are inside the top wire component.

STEP F: After cutting the wire, use your bent chain-nose pliers to squeeze and flatten each end of the cut wire.

Courtesy of Gary Helwig, WigJig.

STEP G: Now, you are ready to add the ear wire finding. Open the loop in your ear wire finding using your bent chain-nose pliers. Connect this loop to the loop in the top wire component made on peg 9. Close the loop.

tip

While you are learning to make this piece, start with 20-gauge wire. The finished earring may look better when made in 18-gauge wire, but it will be easier to learn to make in 20-gauge wire. When you are ready to create your finished earrings using your good wire, half-hard wire will help to make more consistent pieces.

ADDING THE BEADS

STEP A: Using a head-pin jewelry finding, thread one or more beads onto the head pin. For the earrings shown here, we used one 6 mm bead per loop for a total of five 6 mm beads per earring.

STEP B: Make a wrapped bead dangle (see page 28). Connect the wrapped dangle to the loop made in the earring body on peg 1 (page 34).

STEP C: Repeat the process for the loop made on peg 2.

STEP D: Repeat the process for the loop made on peg 4.

STEP E: Repeat the above process for the loop made on peg 6.

STEP F: Repeat the above process for the loop made on peg 7.

Courtesy of Gary Helwig, WigJig.

STEP G: Pick up your earring and hold it at arm's length to admire. This is your finished chandelier earring. Make a second earring following the same steps.

Confetti
Earrings

GATHERING YOUR GOODS

6	lampwork 10 mm to 15 mm beads
4	ivory 4 mm to 6 mm freshwater pearls
4	pink 4 mm to 6 mm freshwater pearls
4	light pink AB 4 mm bicone crystals
4	clear AB 4 mm bicone crystals
10 to 12	various Bali silver 2 mm to 6 mm nuggets or rounds
50	seed beads in a color variety within the palette
	20-gauge sterling silver round wire, dead soft (4 or 5 times your finished length)
	24-gauge sterling silver round wire, dead soft (4 or 5 times your finished length)
2	sterling silver ear wires

TOOLS TO HAVE ON HAND

- Round-nose pliers
- Chain-nose pliers
- Flat-nose pliers
- Wire cutters
- Ruler

Designer: Barbara Markoe
Finished Size: 1¼"
Expense: Less than $50
Level of Expertise: Intermediate
Time to Complete: 1 to 2 hours

STEP A: Start with a 4½" length of 20-gauge wire. This will form the base of your earring. On one end form a small loop using round nose pliers (the smaller the better). With the flat pliers, bend the loop a slight angle to the wire.

STEP B: Loop remaining length through newly created "eye," leaving about 1½" sticking out the top. This is the length that will attach to the ear wire. Decide what shape you want, i.e., round or teardrop, etc. Adjust and shape (you will need to re-adjust at the end).

STEP C: With the 1½" piece, make a small loop with round-nose pliers. Insert ear wire into loop and wire wrap down to "eye" to secure. You should have a plain "hoop" earring. Repeat for earring two.

STEP D: Take about 15" of 24-gauge wire. Start by wrapping the wire three or four times at one end of the hoop. As you continue, start to add beads randomly: A few seeds, a bicone, a pearl, wrapping between each section. It may take a few wraps to get the hang of it. If you run out of wire, simply start another piece in the same manner. These earrings are wrapped two times (forward and back). Clean up ends with wire cutters. Re-adjust shape if necessary.

Designer: Barbara Markoe.

GATHERING
YOUR GOODS

32	tangerine 4 mm crystal bicones
2	natural brass 2¼" Etruscan filigrees
2	natural brass 20 mm earring wires
16	natural brass 1" headpins
16	natural brass 4.5 mm jump rings

TOOLS
TO HAVE ON HAND

- Ergonomic rosary pliers with side cutters
- Ergonomic chain-nose pliers (2 pair)

Designer: Jeanne Holland
Finished Size: 3"
Expense: Under $25
Expertise: Beginner
Time to Complete: An evening

Tangerine Tempest
Chandelier Earrings

The technique of creating a bead drop will give you a basic component that you will use in many designs.

MAKING YOUR BEAD DROPS

String two tangerine 4 mm bicones onto a 1" head pin. Then, make a bead drop following the directions on page 28. Create 16 bead drops in total.

ASSEMBLING YOUR EARRINGS

STEP A: It might help you to review the basic jump ring technique on page 20. Using 4.5 mm jump rings, attach two bead drops to each of the four lower-most openings in the filigree.

STEP B: Using chain-nose pliers, attach your earring wire to the top opening of the filigree.

STEP C: Repeat steps A and B to create your second earring.

Courtesy of Beadazzled. Photography by Cas Webber.

GATHERING YOUR GOODS

4 gm Vermilion red matte Japanese Delica size 11 beads

8" sterling silver wire, dead-soft 20-gauge

10" sterling silver chain (figure-eight)

42 sterling silver ball top headpins

2 sterling silver shepherd's hook with ball ear wires

6 sterling silver 4 mm jump rings

TOOLS TO HAVE ON HAND

- Round-nose pliers
- Chain-nose pliers
- Wire cutter
- Ruler

Chinese Firecracker
Earrings

These beautiful dangling earrings show you how spectacular adding a chain can be to highlight your beads.

Courtesy of Beadazzled. Photography by Cas Webber.

Designer: Kathleen Manning

Finished Size: 4" without earring wires, 4½" with wires

Expense: $25 to $50

Expertise: Intermediate

Time to Complete: An evening

MAKING CHANDELIER SHAPES WITH WIRE

STEP A: Measure and cut four 2" pieces of wire.

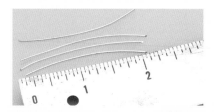

STEP B: Place a 2" wire on round-nose pliers with an inch of wire on each side of the pliers and halfway between the tip and base of the pliers.

STEP C: Holding the pliers in your right hand, cross the wires over each other with left hand to make a loop. Do this on four wires.

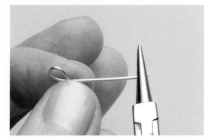

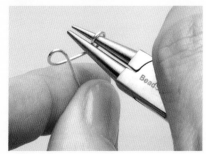

STEP D: Gripping the loop you just made in your left hand, place the pliers on the wire to make side loops, holding the pliers with your palm upward to make the loops by rolling the wire to the left. This makes a loop in one smooth movement. This wire should be halfway between the tip and base of the pliers to make the same size loop. The loop size is determined by where it is rolled on the pliers. The tip makes a small loop; the base a large loop. Turn the wire and do the same on the other side. Repeat on the remaining wires. For headpins on the Firecracker Earrings, the wire will be ¼" long, so wrap ¼" from the tip of pliers.

Courtesy of Beadazzled. Photography by Cas Webber.

OPENING AND CLOSING LOOPS

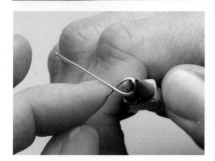

STEP A: Place chain-nose pliers on a jump ring or loop at the "3 o'clock" position (9 for left side) and pull the wire toward you slightly, like opening a gate. Don't pull out!

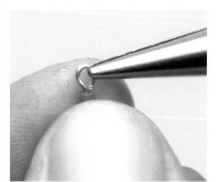

STEP B: Put down the pliers, keeping hold of the loop, and slide wire, chain or earring onto the loop.

STEP C: Close the loop, placing the pliers at 3 o'clock, and push the wire back, like shutting a gate.

> **tip**
>
> If you are left-handed, use your left when instructed to use your right hand. Your hands are your best tools. Be "close" to what you are holding, and you will have more control.

Courtesy of Beadazzled. Photography by Cas Webber.

MAKING THE "FIRECRACKERS"

STEP A: Place nine Delicas on each of 38 of the headpins for dangles. See page 28 for directions on making dangles.

STEP B: Place five Delicas on each of four headpins for links that connect the decorative wire pieces. Cut the ball off the bottom of the beads with the round-nose pliers to make a 90-degree angle. Do this with the 38 headpins.

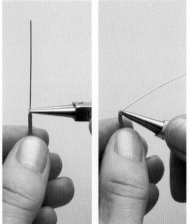

STEP C: Bend the wire on top of these pins, as you will be making loops on each side of the beads.

STEP D: Measure the length of the previously bent wire to make it ¼" long and cut. (See page 40 for wire manipulation for these loops.) Do the same for the four connecting links.

Courtesy of Beadazzled. Photography by Cas Webber.

ASSEMBLING THE PARTS

STEP A: Measure and cut four 1½" chain sections. Measure and cut two 2" chain sections.

STEP B: Attach headpins to the chain: seven each to the 1½" sections, five each to the 2" sections, starting at the end of the chain and working "upward."

STEP C: Attach the chandelier shapes together with bead links.

STEP D: Join the 2" chain with beads to the center loops of the chandelier shapes on the bottom shape, and the two 1½" chains to each side loop with the jump rings. Attach the earring wires to the middle top loop of the chandelier shapes.

Courtesy of Beadazzled. Photography by Cas Webber.

Techniques for Wire Manipulation

The techniques for wire manipulation start with "fittings." Fittings are the magic handmade connectors needed to create wire jewelry. Whether creating a hook and eye clasp, a pendant from a bead or donut, adding chain to your design, or constructing double-spiral "S" connectors, fittings are essential.

Designer: Dotsie S. Mack; Ocean Tide Necklace

Making a Cascade

A cascade is a lovely addition to any piece of jewelry. Use beads of your choice to enhance your own bead and wire jewelry.

STEP A: Cut a 4" sterling silver chain into two pieces, one 1½" long and one 2½" long. Using head pins, attach three 6 mm beads, one 8 mm bead and three 4 mm beads to the shorter sterling silver chain using the simple wrapped loop connectors method below.

STEP B: String one large focal bead and one 2 mm bead onto a head pin. Attach to the bottom of the chain using the wrapped loop method. With head pins, attach your choice of beads, pearls, or crystals, and one large focal bead in the same manner onto the longer sterling silver chain. Attach the two sterling silver chains (cascade) onto a bail loop using the wrapped loop method.

Sue Kwong and Karen Li: Island Princess Necklace.

Simple Wrapped Loop Connectors

STEP A: Cut a piece of wire approximately 1½" longer than desired finished length.

STEP B: Using a flat-nose pliers, bend one end of the wire at a 90-degree angle close to the end of the bead.

STEP C: Using a round-nose pliers, wrap the wire around the pliers making a small loop.

STEP D: Cut away excess wire with wire cutter. Optional: Add jump ring.

STEP E: Close loop using flat-nose pliers.

STEP F: String on desired beads, leaving 1" of remaining wire.

STEP G: Bend wire to a 90-degree angle using flat-nose pliers.

STEP H: Use round-nose pliers to form a second loop.

STEP I: Cut away the excess wire. Add an additional jump ring.

STEP J: Close the loop and attached jump ring with round nose pliers.

STEP K: Continue to add lengths of wire by forming new loops and attaching to the next section with a jump ring.

STEP L: You also can add your clasp to the length using the attached jump rings as connectors.

Wire Wrapping a Pendant

GATHERING YOUR GOODS

- 18-gauge craft wire
- 48 mm olive jade donut

TOOLS TO HAVE ON HAND

- Chain-nose pliers
- Round-nose pliers
- Rosary pliers

Designer: Trish Italia
Green Eggs and Siam

WIRE WRAPPING A DONUT-SHAPED PENDANT

STEP A: Cut a 10" piece of wire.

STEP B: Place the wire behind the donut with 2" showing on top of the donut.

STEP C: Bring the long end of the wire through the hole of the donut from the back and up to the top of donut.

STEP D: Loosely wrap the wire around the stationary wire on top, once or twice, stopping at the front of donut.

STEP E: Bring the wire down and form a freehand loop around the donut hole.

STEP F: Bring the remainder of the wire down, and holding the end of the wire with chain-nose pliers, twist the wire, forming a spiral as loose or tight as you desire.

STEP G: To form a loop on top of the pendant, place the round-nose pliers about ¼" above the wrapped part of the wire. Holding the pliers tightly, twist your wrist toward you. Using your thumb and forefinger, push the wire up and over the pliers, forming the loop.

STEP H: Bring the wire to the front, crossing over the stationary wire and forming a right angle.

STEP I: Wrap the remainder of the wire, forming a coil. Cut away the remainder of wire with a wire cutter.

tip
Remember, it is freeform wrapping, so each project will be a little different.

MAKING A HOOK END FOR A CLASP

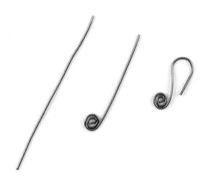

STEP A: Cut a 3" piece of wire for the hook part of the clasp.

STEP B: Hold one end of the wire with chain-nose pliers; form a spiral by twisting your wrist and pushing the wire with your hand.

STEP C: Place the large end of the round-nose pliers ½" above the spiral. With your hand, form the wire around the large end of the pliers.

By further manipulation, you can alter the look of your clasp as shown in the Noe Lani Bracelet below. A chasing hammer was used to flatten the wire.

Designer: Barbara Markoe.

STEP D: Grasp the end of the wire with round-nose pliers, and form a spiral by twisting your wrist and pushing the wire with your hand.

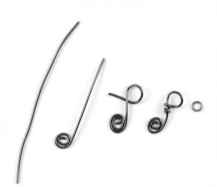

STEP E: Cut a 3" piece of wire for the eye of the clasp.

STEP F: Repeat Step B.

STEP G: Place the small end of the rosary pliers ½" above the spiral. With

your hand, form the wire around the small end of the pliers.

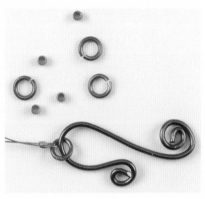

STEP H: Wrap the remainder of the wire, and cut the extra wire with a wire cutter.

MAKING A FLATTENED CLASP

STEP A: Flatten one end of the wire with a chasing hammer and steel bench block.

STEP B: With the tip of the chain-nose pliers, create a loop at the end where the wire is flat.

STEP C: In the back, or largest part of the round-nose pliers, form a loop in the opposite direction from the small loop made previously.

STEP D: Grasp the other end of the wire with the tip of the round- or chain-nose pliers. Have as little of the wire peeking through the end of the pliers as possible. Now, begin coiling the wire. Grasping your developing coil with your chain-nose pliers, continue to coil until you measure 1⅝" from end to end.

STEP E: Grasp the wire next to coil with chain-nose pliers. With your left thumb pressing against the tail of the wire, form a bend. Grasp the loop with a large round-nose pliers and gently urge the wire to rest next to the coil. Partially close the clasp with the round-nose pliers.

STEP F: Use a chasing hammer to flatten the curve of the loop and also the bend at the bottom of the clasp. Open one eye on the bangle and insert clasp through the bottom "V" section. Close the eye.

GATHERING
YOUR GOODS

1	pewter 14 mm side-drilled hole bead
4	garnet 8 mm x 5 mm beads
14"	sterling 2.1 mm rolo chain
4"	sterling 22-gauge wire
4"	sterling 20-gauge wire
1	fancy sterling lobster clasp
1	sterling charm with two holes at each end Make sure one is a larger hole to fit clasp —or use a jump ring.

Tumbling your piece also "work hardens" the sterling for a stronger necklace.

TOOLS
TO HAVE ON HAND

- Round-nose pliers
- Flat-nose pliers
- Wire cutters
- For antique finish (optional):
  Liver of sulfur, steel wool pad extra fine 000, rock tumbler *Caution: Always follow manufacturer's directions when using Liver of Sulphur.
- See more information about the use of liver of sulfur on page 48.

Protect My Heart
Necklace

You can use a simple jump ring in place of the charm to attach the clasp. And, be sure to antique and rub your sterling chain before making this necklace. Tumble it when you are done.

Finished Size: 16"
Expense: $25 to $50
Expertise: Beginner
Time to Complete: An evening
Designer: Sherrie Chapin

Using Chain in Bracelets and Necklaces

PLANNING YOUR NECKLACE

STEP A: There are five sections in this necklace: two ends, two chains and one pendant. The five sections are linked together using the wrapped loop method; see directions on pages 28-30.

STEP B: Cut the rolo chain into two even pieces.

STEP C: Cut the 4" sterling 22-gauge wire into two 2" pieces.

Sherrie Chapin. Courtesy of Blue Moon.

MAKING THE BODY OF THE NECKLACE

STEP A: Add a garnet to one 2" piece of 22-gauge wire and center it. Using flat-nose pliers, bend one end of the wire close to the bead at a 90-degree angle.

Sherrie Chapin. Courtesy of Blue Moon.

STEP B: Place your round-nose pliers at the bent area.

Sherrie Chapin. Courtesy of Blue Moon.

STEP C: Wrap the wire up and around the round-nose pliers to form a wrapped loop. (The wire will be around the top of the pliers.)

Sherrie Chapin. Courtesy of Blue Moon.

STEP D: Add the chain before closing the loop.

Sherrie Chapin. Courtesy of Blue Moon.

STEP E: Make a wrapped loop on the other side of the bead, adding the clasp before closing the loop.

Sherrie Chapin. Courtesy of Blue Moon.

STEP F: Repeat the steps for the other side of the necklace.

ATTACHING THE PENDANT

STEP A: Place a garnet, the pendant and another garnet on the 4" piece of 20-gauge wire.

STEP B: Using flat-nose pliers, create a wrapped loop. Bend one end of the wire close to the bead at a 90-degree angle.

Sherrie Chapin. Courtesy of Blue Moon.

STEP C: Place your round-nose pliers at the bent area.

Sherrie Chapin. Courtesy of Blue Moon.

STEP D: Wrap the wire up and around the round-nose pliers to form a loop. (The wire will be around the top of the pliers.)

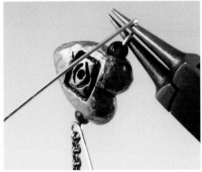

Sherrie Chapin. Courtesy of Blue Moon.

STEP E: Move the loop to the bottom of the round-nose pliers and finish forming a loop. This is the time to add your component (chain, clasp, charm) to the loop as needed.

Sherrie Chapin. Courtesy of Blue Moon.

STEP F: Using flat-nose pliers, grasp the loop and continue wrapping the wire three or four times around itself.

Sherrie Chapin. Courtesy of Blue Moon.

STEP G: Cut away excess wire with wire cutters, and press the end flat with flat-nose pliers.

Sherrie Chapin. Courtesy of Blue Moon.

STEP H: Form another wrapped loop on the opposite wire next to the bead, repeating steps B through G.

Sherrie Chapin. Courtesy of Blue Moon.

ADDING AN ANTIQUE FINISH *(optional)*

Caution: Always follow manufacturer's directions when using Liver of Sulphur.

STEP A: Dip the piece in warm liver of sulfur until just darkened, then rinse. Rub it with steel wool to remove the blackness from the raised parts.

STEP B: Tumble in a tumbler with steel shot, a dash of Dawn soap, and water, three-fourths full, for approximately one hour. Dry.

LIVER OF SULFUR

Precautions: Air destroys liver of sulfur, so you must always keep it in a tightly-sealed closed container. You must also have adequate ventilation when you use it. Do not breathe any of the fumes; **hydrogen sulfide is a poisonous gas!** Any metal that touches this substance will be affected, so use plastic spoons instead. Acid or acid salts, alcohol, or water containing carbon dioxide can affect liver of sulfur adversely or interact with it. Keep it away from your skin or your eyes; **use rubber gloves and safety glasses.** Hydrogen sulfide is an explosive flammable gas so KEEP IT AWAY FROM AN OPEN FLAME.

First Aid: If you inhale the fumes, move to fresh air immediately. If it comes in contact with your skin, flush with plenty of water. If the sulfur contact s the eye, flush with water for at least 15 minutes, then contact an eye doctor. If swallowed, get immediate aid from a physician.

The URL for the MSDS (Material Safety Data Sheet) for this chemical, which you should read, is http://www.jtbaker.com/msds/englishhtml/p5359.htm. It includes general info on disposal, but that may also be regulated state-by-state.

GATHERING
YOUR GOODS

1	aquamarine 15 mm x 12 mm rough-faceted nugget, (side-drilled hole)
13	smooth aquamarine 8 mm x 5 mm rondelles
14"	sterling silver 3.1 mm triple long and short chain
26"	sterling silver 22-gauge wire
6"	sterling silver 20-gauge wire
1	sterling silver 11.3 mm lobster clasp with attached jump ring
1	sterling silver 7 mm to 8 mm bead cap

TOOLS
TO HAVE ON HAND

- Round-nose pliers
- Flat-nose pliers
- Wire cutters
- For antique finish (optional): Liver of sulfur, steel wool pad extra fine 000, rock tumbler
- For more information on liver of sulfur, see page 48.

Aquarius
Necklace

There are nine sections in this necklace: five chain and four aquamarine. The sections are linked together using the wrapped loop method; see pages 28-30 for instructions.

tip

You can use amazonite in place of aquamarine; it's more economical and close to the same color. Tumbling your piece also "work hardens" the sterling for a stronger necklace.

Caution: Always follow manufacturer's directions when using Liver of Sulphur.

Designer: Sherrie Chapin

Finished Size:
Adjustable, 16" to 18"

Expense: $50 to $100

Expertise: Beginner

Time to Complete: A day

CUTTING THE CHAIN AND WIRE

Sherrie Chapin. Courtesy of Blue Moon.

Sherrie Chapin. Courtesy of Blue Moon.

Note: the chain used is made up of short and long links.

STEP A: Cut three pieces of chain to a length of four long links, leaving one short link on both ends.

STEP B: Cut one piece of chain to a length of six long links, leaving one short link on both ends. Cut one piece to a length of three long links with a short link on each end.

STEP C: Cut the 22-gauge sterling wire in 2" pieces for the 13 aquamarine rondelles.

MAKING THE BODY OF THE NECKLACE

STEP A: Wrap three aquamarines together using the wrapped loop method (see pages 28-30). Attach the two end aquamarines to a four-long link chain piece. Wrap another set of three aquamarines to the end of that chain and another chain. This is the center of your necklace.

Sherrie Chapin. Courtesy of Blue Moon.

STEP B: Add three aquamarines to each end of your center necklace piece. Add the three-link chain to one end and the six-link chain to the opposite end.

STEP C: With the last 2" of the 22-gauge wire, add a bead cap to one aquamarine and wrap to the end of the six-link chain. Attach a lobster clasp to the other end using the attached jump ring.

Sherrie Chapin. Courtesy of Blue Moon.

Sherrie Chapin. Courtesy of Blue Moon.

ATTACHING THE PENDANT

STEP A: Using the 6" piece of 20-gauge wire, string the nugget onto the wire, off-center. Bend the wire up both sides of the nugget and twist once.

STEP B: Wrap the short side over, pull the long side straight, and then wrap the short side.

Sherrie Chapin. Courtesy of Blue Moon.

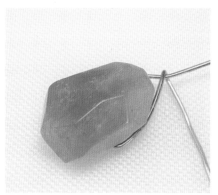

Sherrie Chapin. Courtesy of Blue Moon.

Sherrie Chapin. Courtesy of Blue Moon.

STEP C: Start to form a loop on the long side using the wrapped loop method, pages 28-30.
Attach to the center of the necklace in the middle small link before wrapping the loop closed.
Wrap in a somewhat messy way, up and down, for a full look. Cut the extra wire and tuck it in using flat-nose pliers.

Sherrie Chapin. Courtesy of Blue Moon.

Courtesy of Beadazzled. Photography by Cas Webber.

Pearly Swirly
Bracelet

GATHERING
YOUR GOODS

14	freshwater pearl 5 mm beads
14	sterling silver 5 mm jump rings
4	feet sterling silver 20-gauge wire
14	sterling silver 22-gauge headpins

TOOLS
TO HAVE ON HAND

- Round-nose pliers
- Chain-nose pliers
- Needle-nose pliers
- Wire cutter

Designer: Dotsie S. Mack
Finished Size: 7¼"
Expense: Under $25
Expertise: Intermediate
Time to Complete: A day

MAKING THE CONNECTOR

STEP A: Cut a 3" piece of 20-gauge wire.

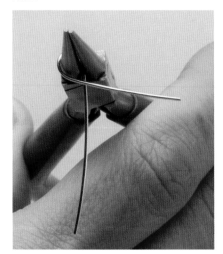

All photos courtesy of Beadazzled. Photography by Cas Webber.

STEP B: Place round-nose pliers in the middle of the wire.

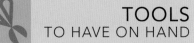

STEP C: Wrap one end around the right base of the tool. Wrap the second end in the `opposite direction around the left side at the base of the tool.

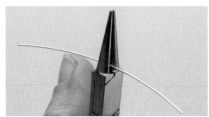

STEP D: Grip the tip of the wire with the tip of round-nose pliers and roll the wire to form a circle.

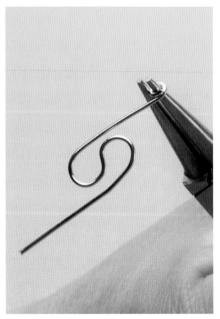

MAKING THE CONNECTOR, *continued*

STEP E: Grip the circle at the base of the chain-nose pliers and begin to spiral inward toward the "S." Stop when the spiral is parallel with the center of the "S."

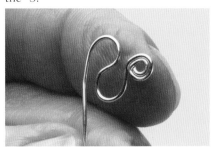

STEP F: Grip the tip of the wire with the tip of round-nose pliers and roll the wire to form a circle on the opposite side of the "S."

STEP G: Grip the circle at the base of the chain-nose pliers and begin to spiral inward toward the "S." Stop when the spiral is parallel with the center of the "S."

Courtesy of Beadazzled. Photography by Cas Webber.

WRAPPING THE LOOP

STEP A: String a pearl on a length of wire. With the tip of your chain-nose pliers, make a sharp right-angle bend at the top of the pearl so that the wire is pointing away from you.

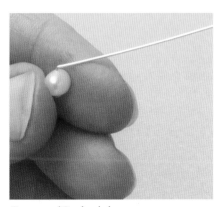

*Courtesy of Beadazzled.
Photography by Cas Webber.*

STEP B: Hold the pearl and wire securely in your non-dominant hand. With your dominant hand, position the bent wire ¼" back from the tip of round-nose pliers and grab the wire ¼" from the bend with the wire pointing away from you. With your palm facing you, rotate your wrist with your dominant hand to roll the wire up and over the top of the tool so that the wire is pointing toward you.

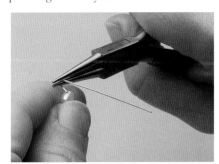

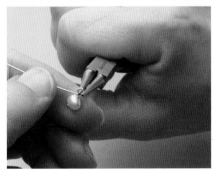

STEP C: Reinsert the wire ¼" back from the tip of the pliers and begin rotating the wire once more, allowing the wire to create an entire circle.

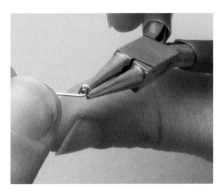

Before you complete the wrap portion of the loop, be sure to attach any components, as this is a secure connection. Grip the loop and rotate the wire in a downward motion until it meets with the pearl. Wrap and clip off excess wire.

Constructing a Double-Spiral "S" Connector

MAKING THE DOUBLE-SPIRAL "S" CHAIN

STEP A: You will use 13 sections of 20-gauge sterling-silver wire, 3" each, to make double spirals (see pages 52-53). Attach a sterling silver soldered jump ring to the top right end of a spiral. Slide the spiral to the center of the "S" so that the jump ring is secured.

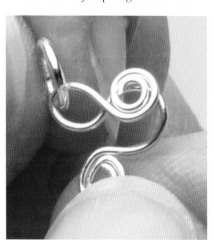

STEP B: Attach a sterling-silver soldered jump ring to the bottom left end of the spiral. Slide the spiral to the center of the "S" so that the jump ring is secured.

STEP C: Attach the jump ring from the bottom left side of the double-spiral "S" to the top of the right side of yet another double spiral.

STEP D: Attach another jump ring to the bottom left of the second spiral to begin creating a chain. Complete this step with all 13 double spirals and 14 jump rings until they form a chain.

ADDING PEARL DANGLES

STEP A: Assemble 14 headpins with one pearl on each.

STEP B: Attach each pearl to the bottom of each jump ring using the wrapped wire loop technique, page 51.

Courtesy of Beadazzled. Photography by Cas Webber.

MAKING THE HOOK-AND-EYE CLASP

STEP A: With the tip of your round-nose pliers, form a small circle at one end of a 3" piece of 20-gauge sterling silver wire.

STEP B: Hold the circle between the jaws of the pliers so that the wire rests at the base of the tool. Rotate the wire around one side of the tool to form a hook.

STEP C: Grip the wire beneath the circle. Make a sharp 90-degree right-angle bend and create a wire-wrap loop.

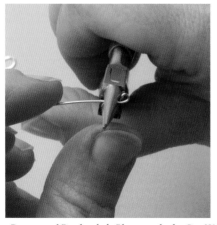
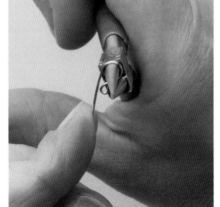
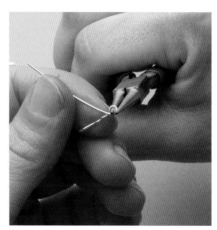

Courtesy of Beadazzled. Photography by Cas Webber.

STEP D: Attach the hook-and-eye clasp to one side of the spiral chain at the jump ring.

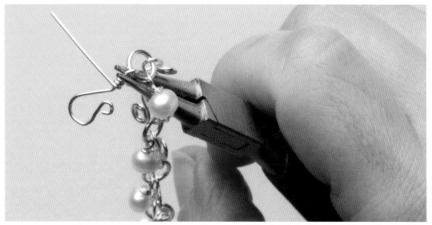

Courtesy of Beadazzled. Photography by Cas Webber.

Ocean Tide
Necklace

CREATING THE DANGLE PENDANT ON CHAIN

STEP A: Cut 2" of 2 mm x 4 mm sterling-silver cable chain.

STEP B: Place one Peruvian opal bead on a headpin and attach it to the center loop of the chain with a wire wrapped loop (see wrapping the loop, page 53).

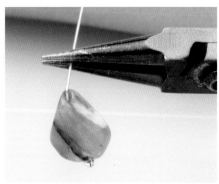

Courtesy of Beadazzled. Photography by Cas Webber.

CREATING THE DANGLE PENDANT ON CHAIN, *continued*

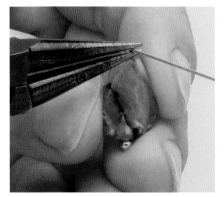

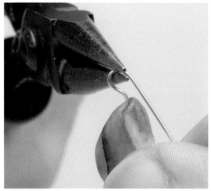

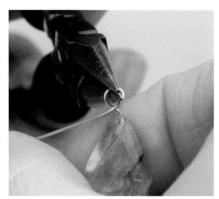

STEP C: Place an olivine crystal on a headpin. Skip one link of chain and then attach it to the chain with a wrapped loop.

STEP D: On the next loop of the chain, place one lentil river stone bead on a headpin and then attach it with a wrapped loop.

STEP E: Place a round Czech glass bead on a headpin, skip one link of chain and attach it with a wrapped loop.

STEP F: Place an indicolite crystal on a headpin. On the second half of the chain (opposite side) skip one link and attach it to the chain with a wrapped loop.

STEP G: On the next loop of the chain, attach one olivine crystal on a headpin to the chain with a wrapped loop.

STEP H: Skip one loop and attach the lentil river stone bead on a headpin and add to the chain using a wrapped loop.

Courtesy of Beadazzled. Photography by Cas Webber.

STEP I: On the next loop of the chain, attach a topaz luster Czech glass bead on a headpin, then attach to the chain with a wrapped loop.

STEP J: Place one river stone lentil on a headpin and begin to create a wire wrapped loop. Before you close the loop, slip on both ends of the chain as well as one oval ring. Complete the wrap.

Courtesy of Beadazzled. Photography by Cas Webber.

BUILDING THE BODY OF THE NECKLACE

STEP A: On a 3" piece of wire, create a wrapped loop and connect the loop to the beaded pendant through the oval jump ring.

All photos courtesy of Beadazzled. Photography by Cas Webber.

STEP B: Place a Peruvian opal nugget on the wire. Create a wrapped loop on the opposite side of the Peruvian opal, but before you close and secure the wrapped loop, add an oval jump ring.

STEP C: On the jump ring that you just attached to the Peruvian opal bead, add a river stone lentil bead with a 3" piece of wire. Before you secure the second loop, attach a sterling silver jump ring on the other side, alternating Peruvian opal and river stone beads.

STEP D: Repeat this process, alternating river stone lentils and Peruvian opals until you have nine beads total on one side, forming a chain of beads.

COMPLETING THE NECKLACE BODY

STEP A: Repeat the section for building the body of the necklace on page 58 to complete the other half of the chain, forming a complete necklace.

STEP B: Assemble 16 of each bead on a headpin: 4 mm bicone olivine crystal, 4 mm bicone indicolite crystal and 4 mm topaz luster Czech glass.

STEP C: Starting above the first Peruvian opal bead, attach one olivine, one indicolite, and one topaz luster bead to each sterling silver soldered oval jump ring. Leave the last oval jump ring free of beads to attach the "S" clasp.

STEP D: Attach a sterling silver "S" clasp to the last oval jump ring on each side of the body of the necklace through the last oval jump rings.

STEP E: Follow the instructions for a hook-and-eye clasp, page 45, and attach it to one side of the chain at the jump ring.

Remember that wire takes the shape of whatever you bend it around. Do not try to use the tip of your pliers when you reinsert to complete a circle, as this will cause your loop to form a teardrop. Find more about jump rings on page 20.

For directions to create a wire wrapped loop, see page 53.

All photos courtesy of Beadazzled. Photography by Cas Webber.

Easy To Use Memory Wire

Memory wire is a fun, quick way to bead with a different look. It comes in a coil like a spring or a Slinky. Today, the coils come in various finishes.

It is called memory wire because it doesn't lose its coil shape even after beads have been added. Memory wire comes in sizes to make necklaces, bracelets and rings. It may come pre-cut in a package or as a coil long enough for several projects. This wire is tough. You will need a heavy-duty (hardware) cutter for memory wire. Do not ruin your good jewelry cutters trying to conquer this task.

When measuring for how much wire to use for bracelets, figure about one-and-a-half loops of wire will expand to about one wrap by the time the beads are threaded on it, depending on the size of the beads.

So, for example, for a bracelet that wraps around your wrist twice, count out a three-loop coil.

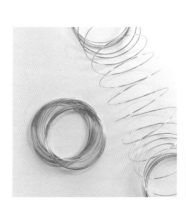

Memory wire shown before beads are strung and after.

Memory Wire Step-by-Step

STEP A: Cut a coil with the number of loops desired.

STEP B: Use pliers to bend one end of the wire into a loop, as shown. This will act as a stop

STEP C: Thread beads onto the memory wire coil, sliding them down to the loop.

STEP D: Make a loop on the other end to secure.

tips

Safety
Protect your hands from the sharp ends of memory wire by wearing gloves. If you can't seem to cut the wire on your own, ask someone for assistance. Use E6000 glue to secure a memory wire bead tip (cap) or bend the end as you would an eyepin (see page 18) to finish.

End Caps
One nice touch is to add dangles to hang off the loops on either end. Another finishing technique, instead of loops on either end, is to glue (E6000) a bead to each end. You can use half-drilled beads or end caps especially made for memory wire.

Decorating with Wire
Memory wire is great for making beaded wraps with lots of uses. The bracelet size can decorate candles, candleholders and vases, and the ring size can make napkin holders and matching wine glass charms. The sky's the limit!

CHAPTER 5

Off the Cuff — Wire-Wrapped Cuffs

Beaded cuffs have recently made a comeback. The ingenuity and beauty of these designs ensure they will be here for a long time.

Courtesy of Beadazzled.
Photography by Cas Webber.

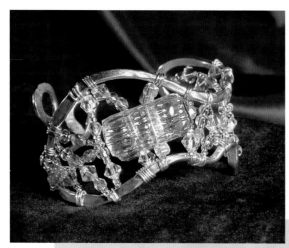

Ronda Terry: Wrist Cuff.

Sandi Webster: Desert Rose Cuff.

Making a Freeform Cuff

Courtesy of Beadazzled. Photography by Cas Webber.

GATHERING YOUR GOODS

- 15" round 12-gauge wire

TOOLS TO HAVE ON HAND

- Black marker
- Ruler
- Mini-file
- Flat-nose pliers
- Round-nose pliers
- Oval bracelet mandrel
- Bench block
- Chasing hammer

Designer: **Cas Webber**

CONSTRUCTING THE CUFF FRAME

STEP A: Use a mini-file to soften the edges of the cut ends of the 12-gauge wire.

Courtesy of Beadazzled. Photography by Cas Webber.

STEP B: With a black marker, mark the wire at 7½".

Courtesy of Beadazzled. Photography by Cas Webber.

STEP C: Measure and mark ¼" on both sides of the 7½" mark.

Courtesy of Beadazzled. Photography by Cas Webber.

STEP D: Make a 90-degree bend at each ¼" mark.

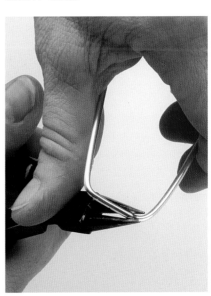

Courtesy of Beadazzled. Photography by Cas Webber.

FORMING THE WIRE ENDS INTO SPIRALS

STEP A: Make a mark 1" from each end of the cuff frame.

Courtesy of Beadazzled.
Photography by Cas Webber.

STEP B: Grip one end of the wire with round-nose pliers and start to rotate the wire outward, away from the frame, forming a loop.

Courtesy of Beadazzled.
Photography by Cas Webber.

STEP C: Grip the loop in the jaw of your flat-nose pliers, and spiral the wire down to the 1" mark.

Courtesy of Beadazzled.
Photography by Cas Webber.

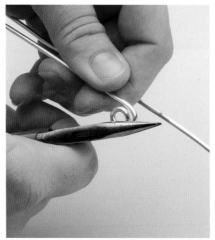

Courtesy of Beadazzled.
Photography by Cas Webber.

STEP D: Grip just above the spiral with flat-nose pliers and make a very slight bend. This will center the spiral at the end.

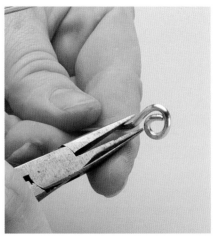

Courtesy of Beadazzled.
Photography by Cas Webber.

STEP E: Repeat the process for the opposite end of the wire.

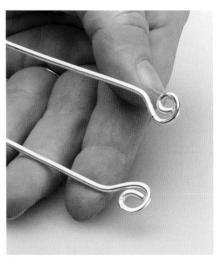

Courtesy of Beadazzled.
Photography by Cas Webber.

HAMMERING SPIRALS ON A BENCH BLOCK

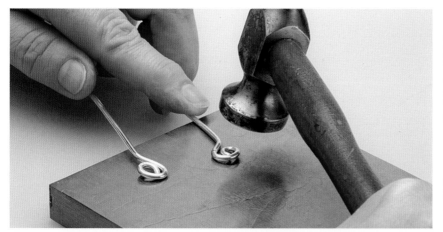

Place both spirals flat on the bench block. Gently let the hammer hit the spirals, ensuring they meet evenly. Finish hammering once both spirals are just flattened.

Courtesy of Beadazzled.
Photography by Cas Webber.

When using a bench block and mandrel, hold the hammer at the base of the handle and allow the weight of the head to strike the wire. Too much force will give an unwanted and uneven texture to the wire. The result of this technique should give you a smooth, even, wire surface. If you desire a textured surface, use the peen to gently tap on the wire.

MAKING WAVES IN THE FRAME

STEP A: Starting from the base on each side of the frame, mark ½" segments.

STEP B: With round-nose pliers, grip at each ½" mark and gently make a slight bend.

SHAPING THE FRAME INTO A CUFF

STEP A: Measure the circumference on the mandrel and mark at 6.5".

STEP B: Position the frame on the mandrel with one wire over the 6.5" mark and one wire under the mark.

STEP C: Mold the wire frame around the mandrel and hold.

STEP D: Gently let the hammer hit the wire frame, ensuring the hammer and wire touch evenly. Finish hammering once the wire frame is just flattened.

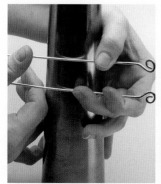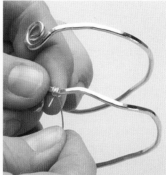

All photos courtesy of Beadazzled. Photography by Cas Webber.

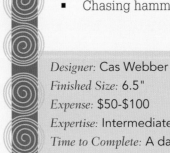

Courtesy of Beadazzled.
Photography by Cas Webber.

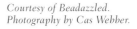

GATHERING YOUR GOODS

50	feet round 24-gauge wire
15"	round 12-gauge wire
6	Strands freshwater pearls, each of a different size and color. Choose one strand of the following shapes with sizes ranging from 3 mm to 8 mm.

Pearl shapes and colors:

13	brown 7 mm x 5 mm keishi beads
22	garnet 6 mm x 4 mm faceted rondelles
13	champagne 8 mm faceted rounds
19	burgundy 5 mm x 4 mm smooth rondelles
19	bronze 4 mm potatoes
12	peach 7 mm potatoes

TOOLS TO HAVE ON HAND

- Black marker
- Ruler
- Mini-file
- Flat-nose pliers
- Round-nose pliers
- Oval bracelet mandrel
- Bench block
- Chasing hammer

Cherry Cordial
Cuff

This project uses freshwater pearls that can be purchased in a wide array of colors, sizes and shapes. Due to the nature of pearl sizes and shapes, this project emphases freeform sizing to create lots of texture and splashes of color.

Designer: **Cas Webber**
Finished Size: 6.5"
Expense: $50-$100
Expertise: Intermediate
Time to Complete: A day

MAKING THE WIRE CUFF FRAME

Follow the directions for making a freeform cuff, pages 63-65.

WIRING BEADS TO THE FRAME

STEP A: Start with 5 feet of 24-gauge wire and begin wrapping just above the spiral on one side of the frame. Make five tight wraps.

Courtesy of Beadazzled.
Photography by Cas Webber.

STEP B: String random beads to equal ¾", or enough to fill the inside of frame, then tightly wrap the opposite side of the frame three times.

Courtesy of Beadazzled.
Photography by Cas Webber.

STEP C: Repeat Step B until you have covered the frame.

Courtesy of Beadazzled.
Photography by Cas Webber.

STEP D: To finish, make five tight wraps.

PROJECT SEQUENCING: At right is the bead key. Below is the order you will use to string the beads. Start from the spirals base, and move top to bottom.

Brown keishi	BK			
Garnet faceted rondelle	GFR			
Champaign faceted round	CFR			
Burgundy smooth rondelle	BSR			
Bronze small potato	BSP			
Peach large potato	PLP			

STRAND	1	BSR	PLP	GFR	BSP
STRAND	2	CFR	BSP	BK	
STRAND	3	BSR	PLP	GFR	BSP
STRAND	4	GFR	BSP	BSR	CFR
STRAND	5	PLP	BK	GFR	BSP
STRAND	6	BSR	BSP	CFR	BSR
STRAND	7	BSP	GFR	GFR	BSP
STRAND	8	BSR	CFR	BK	BSP
STRAND	9	BSR	BSR	BSP	GFR	PLP
STRAND	10	BSP	BSR	BK	GFR	BSP
STRAND	11	CFR	BK	BSP	BSR	
STRAND	12	GFR	PLP	BSR	CFR	
STRAND	13	BSP	BSR	GFR	BK	BSR
STRAND	14	GFR	CFR	BSR	BSP	PLP
STRAND	15	PLP	BSR	BK	GFR	BSP
STRAND	16	GFR	BSP	BSR	CFR	GFR
STRAND	17	BSP	BK	GFR	BSP	BK
STRAND	18	PLP	CFR	BSR	PLP	
STRAND	19	BSP	GFR	GFR	BSP	BK
STRAND	20	BK	GFR	BSR	CFR	
STRAND	21	BSP	PLP	GFR	BSP	BSP
STRAND	22	BSR	BSR	CFR	BK	
STRAND	23	BSR	PLP	GFR	GFR	BSP
STRAND	24	CFR	BSR	PLP		
STRAND	25	BSP	BSR	CFR	GFR	

Courtesy of Sandra Webster.

Desert Rose
Copper Cuff

The instructions and pictures accompanying this design are meant only to show you how you can create a similar bracelet. You will have to provide your own creativity and select the beads and supplies that you wish to use. The possibilities are endless. Bracelets in both copper and sterling silver can be made in many different themes – aquatic, garden, Southwest, modern – whatever suits you. The key is to make each cuff unique and individual.

GATHERING
YOUR GOODS

* Handmade copper cuff with three loops, 2" wide

1 cream 1" tea rose

1 strand turquoise 8 mm to 10 mm side-drilled nuggets

2 vintage carved-ivory 7 mm to 8 mm beads

30-40 vintage bone or ivory 4 mm to 5 mm rondelles

8-10 jungle stripe ⅝" Bohemian glass leaves

Beige pearlized glass seed beads

22-gauge copper wire

* Sandra Webster Jewelry, see Resource Guide.

TOOLS
TO HAVE ON HAND

- Side cutter
- Round-nose pliers
- Drill

Designer: Sandra Webster

Finished Size: Cuff is 2" wide and is adjustable

Expense: $25 - $50

Expertise: Intermediate

Time to Complete: A day

tip

Add the larger beads to the bracelet first, filling in spaces with smaller beads.

SIDE-TO-SIDE TECHNIQUE

STEP A: Drill through the backside of the flower (side-to-side) so that you can easily run wire through it. Cut about 7" of copper wire and run it through the flower. You will be running ends of the wire through loops on the bracelet.

STEP B: Do the same thing with the beads. Run wire through the beads and wire wrap the loops or other beads that have already been attached to the bracelet. Add a coiled decorative end for interest.

STEP C: Take one end of the wire and wrap it around the loop closest to the flower. Run the other end of the wire through one of the other loops on top of the bracelet. Add some nuggets close to the flower and wire wrap them around the flower.

STEP D: Add wire and wrap it to the loops, or whatever you can attach it to. Throughout the process of making the bracelet, add beads — take away beads — whatever suits your taste. The wiring techniques are simple, and you will probably create some new ones of your own!

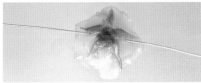

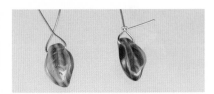

All photos courtesy of Sandra Webster.

TOP-WRAP TECHNIQUE

Another method to attach wire to beads is to wire-wrap top-drilled beads and top-drilled leaves. Always allow at least 7" of wire when you are attaching beads. After you have run the wire through a loop on the cuff or through the mass of wire already in place beneath some beads, you can attach another bead to the end of the wire. Leave about ¾" of wire, and coil it tightly against the bead.

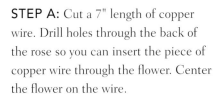

STEP A: Cut a 7" length of copper wire. Drill holes through the back of the rose so you can insert the piece of copper wire through the flower. Center the flower on the wire.

STEP B: Insert the ends of the wire through two of the loops on the bracelet. Wrap one end of the wire around the loop closest to the flower. Add several turquoise nuggets. Wrap the wire around the flower again to tighten. Use round-nose pliers to coil the remaining end of the wire down to the base of the flower where it will not be seen when the bracelet is finished.

STEP C: String six or seven of the nuggets on 7" of copper wire. Wrap the wire around the rose and run the ends of the wire through the loop closest to the rose. You don't have to completely encircle the rose with the nuggets — you will fill in empty spaces with leaves or other beads later. Tighten and twist the wire ends together.

STEP D: Continue adding beads, attaching some to the other loops and also to beads that are already secured on the bracelet. Try to keep as much of the wire hidden as possible, working it down under the beads. You do not want a mass of wire showing.

Rings

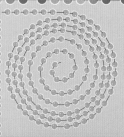

Make a flashy ring with movement that takes full advantage of the beauty and shine of crystal beads.

VARIATIONS

• *Use larger stones or even pearls in 6 mm to 8 mm sizes. The larger the stones, the more the ring "fills in." The same technique can be used for bracelets created for this purpose. Attaching clusters of beads to a chain can also be used to make a beautiful necklace, belt, keychain, or other type of accessory – let your creativity run wild!*

Cha Cha
Bling Ring

Try using an assortment of interesting Austrian crystals, glass pearls, and silver findings. They make beautiful alternatives! Rings available on the Web, including eBay, also have the loops you need to wrap the wires around. Look for rings that have interesting open work that you can use instead of the raised loops. Try headpins with attached beads, or, use standard headpins and string a single tiny round bead before each crystal to simulate the look of the ring in this project.

21	assorted 4 mm Swarovski crystals in colors of your choice
21	silver 3 mm round beads (optional)
	Ring with 1, 2 or 3 loops (or notches) – known as a "Cha Cha" ring
21	sterling silver 1½" headpins with ball tips

TOOLS
TO HAVE ON HAND

- Round-nose pliers
- Chain-nose or flat-nose pliers
- Side cutters

Designer: Ilene Baranowitz
Finished Size: 7¼"
Expense: Under $25
Expertise: Beginner
Time to Complete: An evening

CREATING DANGLING CRYSTALS

STEP A: Place one crystal on the headpin. Place the optional silver beads on top of the crystal.

STEP B: Fold a bend into the wire just above the final bead on the headpin—either the crystal or the optional silver bead.

STEP C: Using the round-nose pliers, create a loop just above the bend, forming a complete circle. (See the wrapped loop method, pages 28-30.)

STEP D: Run the end of the headpin through one of the notches on the ring until the loop you have created is resting inside the notch.

ATTACHING THE DANGLES

STEP A: Holding the pin steady against the notch with the chain- or flat-nose pliers, use your other hand to wrap the end of the pin back around the base. The wrap will be placed just above the bead (or beads) and below the bend.

STEP B: Wrap two or three times close to each subsequent wrap, pulling tightly to secure.

STEP C: Cut the excess wire close to the wraps.

STEP D: Provide a smooth finish by using the chain-nose pliers to squeeze the end flat against the other wraps. Feel for any rough edges and squeeze further to remove these.

STEP E: Repeat for each of the additional crystals, dividing the crystal dangles evenly on each of the notches.

GATHERING YOUR GOODS

1	light-blue 6 mm druk glass round
1	light-blue 4 mm druk glass round
1	clear aurora borealis 4 mm glass round
1	white opaque 4 mm aurora round
2	clear transparent aurora borealis 4 mm x 4 mm cubes
1	ivory opaque 4 mm x 4 mm cube
1	clear 6 mm faceted crystal round
1	light-blue transparent 6/0 round
22"	dark-blue wire

TOOLS TO HAVE ON HAND

- Needle-nose pliers
- Rosary pliers

Designer: Unknown
Finished Size: Varies
Expense: Under $25
Expertise: Beginner
Time to Complete: A day

Train Wreck
Ring

CREATING THE WIRE RING

STEP A: Cut 20" of wire and bend the wire in half.

STEP B: Using a wine cork or small bead bottle, wrap the wire around the cork to form a complete circle. For a stronger ring, continue circling the object completely to form two loops.

STEP C: Make a full twist where the wire comes together at the base of the loops to secure the loops in place.

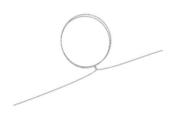

STEP D: Wrap one wire end from front to back through the ring. Continue wrapping in the same direction until you have three wraps away from the center. Then, wrap the second wire end from back to front through the ring and continue wrapping away from the center (the wire will be going in the opposite direction of the first wire).

ADDING YOUR BEADS

STEP A: String the first bead onto the wire. Continue feeding the wire through the ring in the same direction, but start having the wraps move back toward the center of the ring.

STEP B: String one or two beads onto the wire with each wrap.

STEP C: As you fill in from both sides, see if there are any gaps and fill with additional beads and wrap.

STEP D: Bring both wires to the center and twist to secure. Cut off excess wire, if necessary, and twist the ends of the wire into curls using rosary pliers. Tuck curls into the beads.

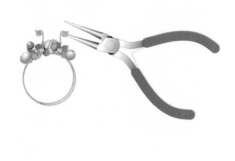

Transform basic bags and accessories into bling beauties, including snappy cell phone cases and handbags, using inexpensive acrylic rhinestones, second-hand bags and the instructions in this innovative book, *Create Your Own Bling*, by Ilene Baranowitz.

create your own
Bling
add glamour to your favorite accessories

GATHERING
YOUR GOODS

1	red 8 mm miracle bead
1	brown 8 mm miracle bead
5	glass 4 mm fire-polished beads
18"	sterling silver 18-gauge wire
4"	sterling silver 22-gauge wire

TOOLS
TO HAVE ON HAND

- Ring mandrel
- Ruler
- Wire cutter
- Chain-nose pliers
- Round-nose pliers

Designer: Kathleen Manning
Finished Size: 3"
Expense: Under $25
Expertise: Beginner
Time to Complete: An evening

Rob Roy
Cocktail Ring

The Rob Roy Cocktail Ring is so easy to make, you can create it on one evening. So fancy — it is fit for a ball!

Practice with inexpensive plated wire before you make your final version.

You can adjust the space between the spirals to change the look. Make the wire longer for larger spirals!

WRAPPING THE WIRE

STEP A: Cut the 18-gauge wire into three 6" pieces. Hold the three wires together at the center (3" on each side). This is where you will wrap them with the 22-gauge wire.

STEP B: Place the 22-gauge wire in the center; wrap around the three wires two times to your right side, and then two times to your left side (you will be wrapping from the center out).

STEP C: Cut the ends off of the wrapped 22-gauge wire. With chain-nose pliers, push the wrapped wire together to make it tighter.

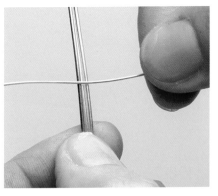 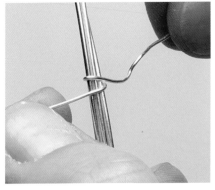 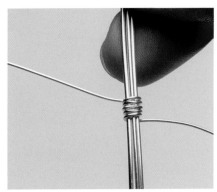

Courtesy of Beadazzled. Photography by Cas Webber.

MAKING THE RING WITH A MANDREL

STEP A: Choose your ring size. With 18-gauge wire, the size may widen, so if you want a 6½ , wrap it at size 6.

STEP B: Hold the mandrel between your knees or put it in a vise. Use both hands to wrap around the mandrel.

STEP C: Twist the wires in front of the mandrel where they meet, just like you would twist a twist-tie on a plastic bag. Pull as tight as you can to keep the ring shape.

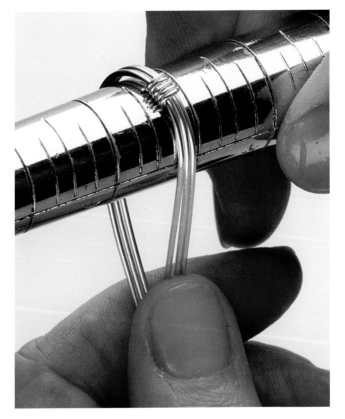

Courtesy of Beadazzled. Photography by Cas Webber.

Courtesy of Beadazzled. Photography by Cas Webber.

ADDING BEADS AND MAKING SPIRALS

STEP A: Add the beads, one at a time. After you add the bead, secure the end of the wire by making a spiral.

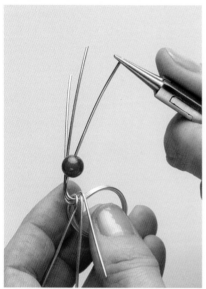

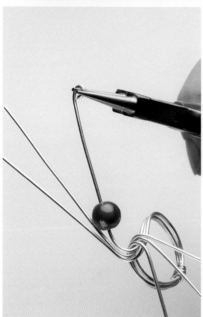

Courtesy of Beadazzled.
All photography by Cas Webber.

STEP B: Using the narrow tip of the round-nose pliers, bend the wire to make a small loop. This will be the center of your spiral. Think of the direction you move your pen when drawing a spiral — wire works the same way.

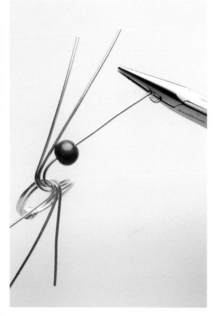

STEP C: Grip the loop with your right hand, using the chain-nose pliers. The wire should be facing out on the left side of the pliers.

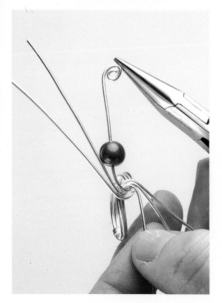

STEP D: Pull the wire toward you to start the spiral. With your left hand, open the pliers, so you can move the wire back to the top. Continue pulling toward you to make the spiral. It gets easier as you go along. Keep doing that until you have reached your desired size.

tip

If you are left-handed, use your left hand instead of your right. Practice, practice, practice! Knowing just a few moves in wire manipulation well, will enable you to do a great many projects!

CHAPTER 7

Coiling Gizmo Basics

Courtesy of LeRoy Goertz, Coiling Gizmo. Photography by Dave Sharp.

LeRoy Goertz's passion is creating. That creativity comes from his working in multiple mediums. Over the course of his life, he has worked in construction, built furniture, blown glass, and created lost-wax castings in silver and bronze. His curiosity about how things are made led him to explore making beads with wire and then to his invention of the Coiling Gizmo. He's now manufacturing, distributing and teaching Gizmo-ing around the country.

The Coiling Gizmo basic system by LeRoy Goertz revolutionized the method for coiling wire by using a chuck, a hollow shaft and a crank. On its heels came the Econo Winder Gizmo. While this system is very affordable, the length of coil produced is limited to the rod's length. Now, the ultimate Deluxe Gizmo allows you to coil much longer lengths, so it's a much better value. Once you understand the basic concept, it's easy to begin making coiled beads to add to your jewelry creations.

TOOLS
TO HAVE ON HAND

- Chain-nose pliers
- Round-nose pliers
- Flush cutter

tip

Begin with copper wire and get a feel for it before moving to precious metals. You can use an assortment of gauges. With sterling, try starting with a 20-gauge wire. You can use the same 20-gauge wire for a bead core, or you can use a 16- or 18-gauge wire.

Understanding Wire Gauge

Wire and metals that come in sheets are measured with the term "gauge." The higher the number, the thinner the metal. For example, a 6-gauge wire is .162" thick and a 20-gauge wire is .032" thick.

Safety Tip
The tools described here seem harmless; however, it is highly recommended that you wear safety glasses when using them. Tools can break and send metal flying.

Courtesy of LeRoy Goertz, Coiling Gizmo.
Photography by Dave Sharp.

A Note About Flush Cutters

Know how to work with your tools first. A flush cutter makes only one part of the cut flush. The wire on the right has a diamond shape. The one on the left has a flush cut.

Plan your cutting so that the flush part of the cut is being used on the jewelry piece you are working on.

Note: See more information about cutting wire on page 16.

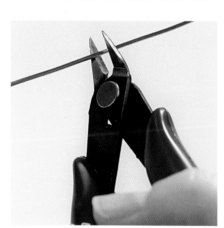

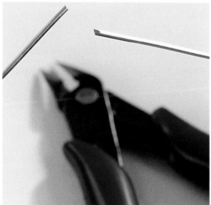

Courtesy of LeRoy Goertz, Coiling Gizmo.
Photography by Dave Sharp.

Wire Cutting Techniques

Cutting wire may seem to be obvious, but it requires education and experience. Jewelry wire cutters, called flush cutters, are made to cut wire leaving one side flush or flat and the opposite side sharp or pointed. The cutters have one flat side and one beveled side. The wire cut on the flat side of the cutter will be left with a flush or flat end. The wire cut on the beveled side of the cutter will be left with a sharp or pointed end. The important thing in making jewelry is that the wire in your finished jewelry must have the flat or flush ends instead of sharp ends. By orienting the flat jaw of your flush cutter toward your finished piece, this can be easily accomplished. **Safety tip:** *When cutting wire, try to contain both ends of the cut wire; otherwise one end may fly up and cause an injury. Wear safety glasses.*

Courtesy of Gary Helwig, WigJig.

Flush   *Sharp*

Using the Econo Winder

MAKING A WIRE COIL

STEP A: Use a 20-gauge or thinner wire. Wire often comes in coils and you need to keep your coil from getting tangled. You can put it on the floor, but put it around something like a quart jar or a metal thermos.

STEP B: Take the end of the wire and push it through the eye of the cranking rod. Then wrap the end of the wire around the eye.

STEP C: Insert the thin crank into the two smallest holes of the bracket frame and begin to crank. Notice how the right thumb is placed over the wire and against the bracket. As you crank, the wire will automatically feed itself and produce a coil spring.

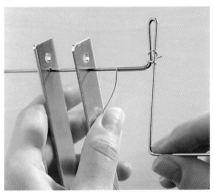

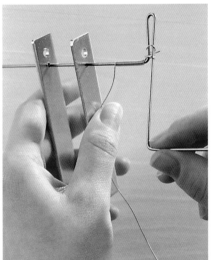

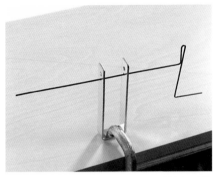

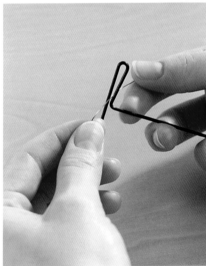

STEP D: Continue cranking until you run out of space on the crank rod. (You can make shorter coiled lengths for smaller beads.)

STEP E: SEE THE SAFETY TIP BELOW. Snip the wire on the right side of the crank at the beginning of the coil, then pull the coil spring off. Look at the end of the spring that you just snipped. Make one more snip to make it look good. Insert the tip of the cutters into the spring. You want to snip just one wire. Remember, the flush side is toward the coils.

Courtesy of LeRoy Goertz, Coiling Gizmo.
All photography by Dave Sharp.

Safety Tip
The tools described here seem harmless; however, it is highly recommended that you wear safety glasses when using them. Tools can break and send metal flying.

STEP F: Warning: You don't want little pieces of metal to fly off when you cut, so cover the whole thing with your hand before snipping the wire (**E**). Now go to the left end of the coil and snip the long wire from that end (**F**). Note: Wear a good pair of safety glasses.

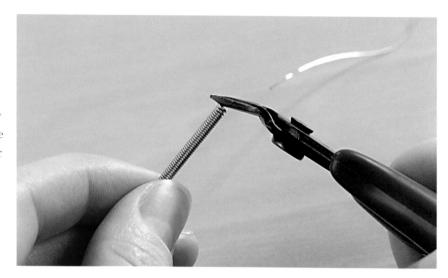

STEP G: Slip a core wire into the coil spring. It can be the same gauge as you are using or thicker. For this wire bead, a core wire of 20-gauge or thicker is recommended. (Thinner core wires make beads of this size too soft.)

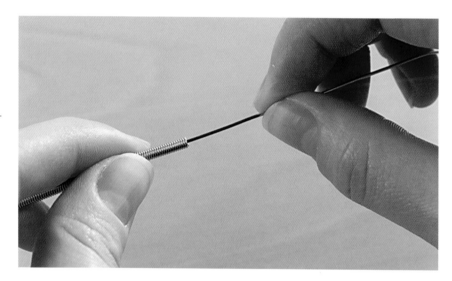

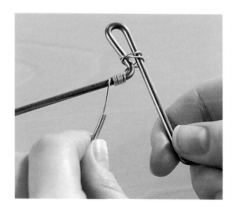 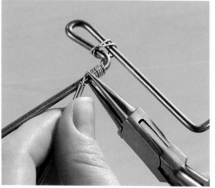 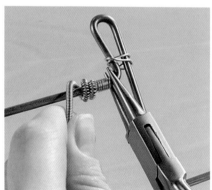

Courtesy of LeRoy Goertz, Coiling Gizmo.
All photography by Dave Sharp.

STEP H: Take the thicker cranking rod, and thread the core wire into the eye, as you did previously. Begin to crank. You will note how the core wire slips through the coil spring as you crank. If you have spaces in the coil that you just made, take your chain-nose pliers and push the wire toward the crank.

CREATING A DOUBLE COIL

STEP A: The coil spring isn't going to want to go over the crank rod by itself. With a little practice, you will find that you can assist it by pushing the spring over the rod with your left hand. Once it catches, it will coil by itself just by letting the spring slip through the fingers of your hand.

Once you have finished coiling the coil spring, you will come to the bare core wire. Match the number of coils on the left end with the number on the right.

STEP B: Snip the wire on the right. Go into the coil and snip as you did earlier. Remove the long wire on the other end. Now, you have a double-coil cylinder bead.

Courtesy of LeRoy Goertz, Coiling Gizmo. All photography by Dave Sharp.

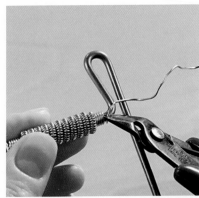

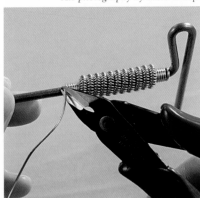

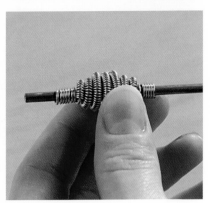

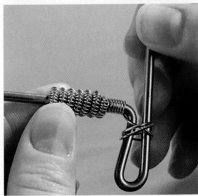

STEP C: You can slip another wire into this bead and make eyes on each end of the wire. You can choose to leave the bead in the shape of a cylinder, or put that cylinder back onto the crank rod, and, by twisting the bead, make it have an oval shape in the middle, as you see in the picture.

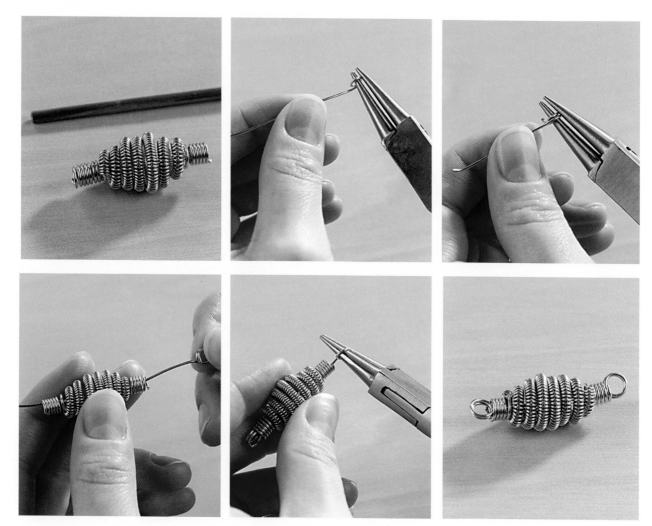

Courtesy of LeRoy Goertz, Coiling Gizmo.
All photography by Dave Sharp.

Have pre-coiled lengths of various gauge wires on hand so you can cut the size coil needed as you assemble your piece. This saves loads of time. Approximately 10" of wire in small gauges will make an inch of coil. When making coils, use a mandrel (or rod) size that best reflects the base you will be working on – such as 14 gauge or 12 gauge.

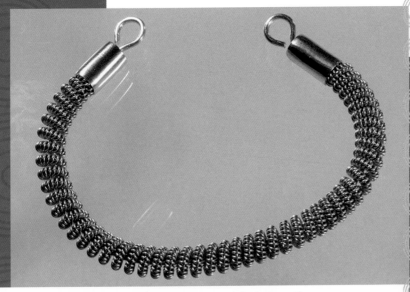

Courtesy of LeRoy Goertz, Coiling Gizmo. Photography by Dave Sharp.

Simple Coiled
Bracelet

Use the following to figure out wire usage for one foot of 20-gauge wire:
- *Around a 9-gauge rod = 1"*
- *Around a 14-gauge rod = 1⅜"*
- *Around a 16-gauge rod = 1¾"*
- *18" coil with 14-gauge rod for second wrapping = 6¾"*
- *22" with 14-gauge rod for the first wrapping and 9 gauge for the second = 7"*

GATHERING
YOUR GOODS

Sterling silver 20-gauge wire

Sterling silver 18-gauge wire

Sterling silver 16-gauge wire

End caps

TOOLS
TO HAVE ON HAND

- Professional Deluxe Coiling Gizmo
- Flush cutter
- Chain-nose pliers
- Round-nose pliers
- Welding rods

Designer: LeRoy Goertz

Expense: Under $25

Expertise: Intermediate

Time to Complete: Thirty minutes for a beginner; 10 to 15 minutes with practice

SETTING UP THE GIZMO

To set up the Professional Deluxe Coiling Gizmo, insert a welding rod that is about 17 gauge in diameter into the chuck. The tail of the rod is inserted into the tail-stock. This rod should be about 24" long. Lay a marking wire on the table about 20" from the tip of the chuck.

Courtesy of LeRoy Goertz, Coiling Gizmo. Photography by Dave Sharp.

STARTING THE WIRE

STEP A: Secure the wire. Make a 90-degree bend on the end of a 20-gauge wire so that the bend is about ¾" from the end of the wire. Then, insert the wire into the space between the jaws of the chuck.

STEP B: Coil about six revolutions. Guide the wire through your forefinger and thumb.

Courtesy of LeRoy Goertz, Coiling Gizmo. Photography by Dave Sharp.

FINISHING THE COIL

STEP A: In the Gizmo kit you will find a funny-looking two-piece wooden clamp with leather jaws. This tool is used to guide the wire. The wire slips through the jaws, allowing you to feed the wire steadily and produce evenly-spaced coils. Clamp this tool to the wire.

STEP B: Continue coiling until you reach the wire marker that you placed on the table.

Courtesy of LeRoy Goertz, Coiling Gizmo.

STEP C: Grab the chuck and loosen it. Slide the welding rod out of it, and remove it from the chuck. Pull it out of the tail-stock. Slide the spring off of the welding rod.

STEP D: Place the tip of your flush cutter inside the spring and snip off the twisted ends of the spring.

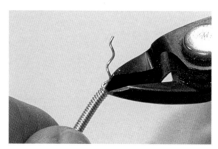

Courtesy of LeRoy Goertz, Coiling Gizmo.

THE SECOND COILING

Courtesy of LeRoy Goertz, Coiling Gizmo.

STEP A: Place an 18-gauge wire into the spring.

STEP B: Put a thick 14-gauge welding rod into the chuck.

STEP C: Make a right-angle bend on the end of the 18-gauge wire and slip it between the jaws of the chuck. Crank six or seven times.

STEP D: To wind the coil spring around the wire, pinch the core wire just below the coil spring. Start cranking and the coil spring will begin winding around the rod.

STEP E: Crank until there is no coil spring left; make another six or seven coils with the bare core wire so that it matches the other end of the piece.

Courtesy of LeRoy Goertz, Coiling Gizmo.

COMPLETING THE BRACELET

STEP A: Slip a 16-gauge wire through the coil that you just made, then slip an end cap onto the wire. Make a right-angle bend about 5/16" from the end.

STEP B: Take round-nose pliers and make an eye loop at the end of the 16-gauge wire using the fattest part of the pliers. Grasp the wire.

STEP C: On the opposite end of the bracelet, place an end cap on the wire. Snip the wire 5/16" from the end of the bracelet.

STEP D: Make another eye loop to match the one that you just made. It's a bracelet with two eyes waiting for their clasp to be added.

Courtesy of LeRoy Goertz, Coiling Gizmo.

Variation of the Simple Coiled Bracelet.

Twisted Coiled Bracelet

Courtesy of LeRoy Goertz, Coiling Gizmo. Photography by Dave Sharp.

Basic coiling is easy to do with a coiling device. Follow the directions on page 80. Hold your wire tight as you coil, so you have nice tight coils. Practice getting tight coils with 18- or 20-gauge wire.

GATHERING
YOUR GOODS

18-, 20-, 22- and 24-gauge silver and copper wire

TOOLS
TO HAVE ON HAND

- Flush wire cutter
- Coiling Gizmo or other coiling machine
- Mandrels for coiling, sizes 12 through 20 gauge (Some are supplied with the Coiling Gizmo. You can supplement them with steel rods in various gauges from a local hardware store.)
- Power drill (optional)
- 2" decorative hook (for twisted wire)

Designer: **LeRoy Goertz**
Out of Africa Bracelet

MAKING TWISTED COILS

STEP A: For beautiful twists, this technique is a must. Insert your 2" decorative hook into the end of the drill where a bit would go. Tighten; now you have a drill with a hook coming out of it.

STEP B: Take about five feet of 18-gauge copper wire. Bend it in half.

STEP C: Secure the two loose ends together in a vise grip. Tighten.

STEP D: Hook the middle section onto your decorative hook.

STEP E: Slowly turn your drill on and watch your wire begin to twist. Keep it fairly taut while you drill.

STEP F: When you've twisted your wire to a desired twist, simply release it from the vise and slip it off the hook. It will be long and straight.

STEP G: Go back to basic coiling and follow the directions. You should now have a beautiful twisted coil

CAUTION: Follow manufacturer's directions when using a power drill. Be sure to wear safety glasses.

Try an inexpensive wire such as copper when you begin to practice. It is available in most hardware stores.

Work with as long a piece of wire as you can handle when making twisted coil. By the time you twist and coil, you end up with a small piece.

GATHERING YOUR GOODS

2	lampwork 8 mm to 10 mm beads
4	silver ball 3 mm beads
4	small Bali 3 mm beads
4	Bali ¼" tube beads
8	Bali 6 mm daisy beads
4	Bali 10 mm beads
10"	silver wire, 20-gauge, cut into two 5" pieces
2"	coiled silver 20-gauge wire, cut into four ½" lengths, coiled on 16/18-gauge mandrel (see Coiling Technique, page 80)
2	silver ear wires

TOOLS TO HAVE ON HAND

- Round-nose pliers
- Small round-nose pliers (available at most jewelry suppliers for small gauge work)
- Small flat-nose pliers (available at most jewelry suppliers for small gauge work)
- Chasing hammer
- Bench block or anvil

Designer: **Barbara Markoe**

Finished Size: **Approximately 1¼" without ear wire**

Expense: **Under $25**

Expertise: **Intermediate**

Time to Complete: **An evening**

Emerald Dynasty
Earrings

PREPPING THE BASE WIRE

STEP A: Blunt cut both ends of your 5" 20-gauge wire.

STEP B: Repeat with the next piece.

STEP C: In one end of each wire, make an eye with small round-nose pliers. Make it as small as possible.

STEP D: Gently hammer each eye to give it a flat appearance and "harden" the wire.

STRINGING BEADS AND COILS

Begin "stringing" your beads and coiled wire pieces onto your 5" wire using the beading sequence at right.

BEADING SEQUENCE

3 MM SILVER BALL

3 MM SMALL BALI

¼" TUBE BALI

6 MM DAISY

½" SILVER COIL

6 MM DAISY

10 MM BALI

LAMPWORK BEAD

10 MM BALI

6 MM DAISY

½" SILVER COIL

6 MM DAISY

¼" TUBE BALI

3 MM SMALL BALI

3 MM SILVER BALL

WORKING THE WIRE

STEP A: When you have finished your stringing, take your flat-nose pliers and bend the eye end at a 90-degree angle.

STEP B: Insert wire from other end through eye and make a 90-degree bend. You should now have some thing that looks like a circle. Don't worry about adjusting; you can do that after everything is secure.

CREATING THE END EYE

STEP A: Clip off the remaining wire so that you have about 1½" from the top of the earring.

STEP B: About ¼" up from the top of the earring, make a small eye with your round-nose pliers.

STEP C: Insert the ear wire into the loop and wrap it down to the top of the earring. Clip the end and secure. Repeat for the other earring.

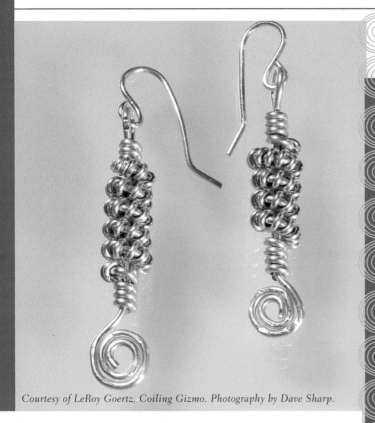

Courtesy of LeRoy Goertz, Coiling Gizmo. Photography by Dave Sharp.

GATHERING
YOUR GOODS

Welding rod

One ounce sterling silver 24-gauge dead-soft wire

One ounce sterling silver 20-gauge dead-soft wire

TOOLS
TO HAVE ON HAND

- Professional Deluxe Coiling Gizmo
- Round-nose pliers
- Chain-nose pliers
- Flush cutter
- Side cutter or jeweler's saw
- Ruler
- Cup bur, pin vise (optional, for ear wires)

Designer: LeRoy Goertz
Finished Size: 2" to 3", without ear wire
Expense: Under $25
Expertise: Beginner
Time to Complete: Half an hour to an hour

Celtic Coil
Earrings

These earrings are beautifully coiled but there are precautions you need to take when cutting a rod. Use a side cutter, or cut the rod with a jeweler's saw. Flush cutters were designed for soft metals like gold, silver, copper or brass. Side cutters were designed for steel and iron.

PREPARING THE WELDING ROD

STEP A: Cut a 3" piece of welding rod that is about a 17-gauge thickness.

STEP B: There will be a burr on the cut parts. You will need to file or sand off that burr so that a coil spring will slip off when you cut it.

MAKING THE COIL SPRING

STEP A: Push the short welding rod into the Coiling Gizmo's chuck so that about 1½" sticks out of the chuck.

STEP B: Make two coil springs using 24-gauge wire; follow the directions on page 84 for making coiled bracelets. Coil up to the end of the welding rod and pull the coil spring off the rod.

THE SECOND COILING

Slip a 20-gauge wire into the spring. Use the same short piece of welding rod that you used to make the coil spring. Follow the directions for making the coil spring bracelet on page 84. Make about four coils with the bare core wire on each end. Snip the ends.

Courtesy of LeRoy Goertz, Coiling Gizmo. Photography by Dave Sharp.

MAKING CELTIC COILS

STEP A: Slip a 20-gauge wire into the bead and make a small eye using the tip of the round-nose pliers.

STEP B: Use chain-nose pliers to finish the coiling.

STEP C: Make an eye on the other end of the bead. Making ear wires

Courtesy of LeRoy Goertz, Coiling Gizmo. Photography by Dave Sharp.

MAKING EAR WIRES

Making your own ear wires enables you to design a unique shape. The best wire for these is 20 gauge, but make sure that the ends of the wires have been filed down so that there are no rough points. A cup bur that is secured in a pin vise works well for this.

STEP A: Cut two pieces of 20-gauge wire. Hold both of them in your hand.

STEP B: Take your round-nose pliers and make eyes on the ends of the wires. Use the smaller end of your pliers.

STEP C: Using the wider part of the pliers, make a loop.

STEP D: Optional: Give your wires a little bend at the other end.

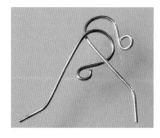

STEP E: Open the eyes of the ear wires a little and slip on beads.

tip

This is more wire than you need for this project. However, buying in one-ounce quantities will give you the best price.

Save all of the scrap pieces of wire when you are working with precious metals. You can sell them to a refiner who will melt them down and make new wire or other products.

To make multiple units: If you want to make 10 pairs of earrings, you might start by making 20 coil springs. Then, follow all of the steps sequentially, completing each step 20 times. Keep going until you have gone through all of the steps with the 20 setups. You will save time by completing each task before changing the setup.

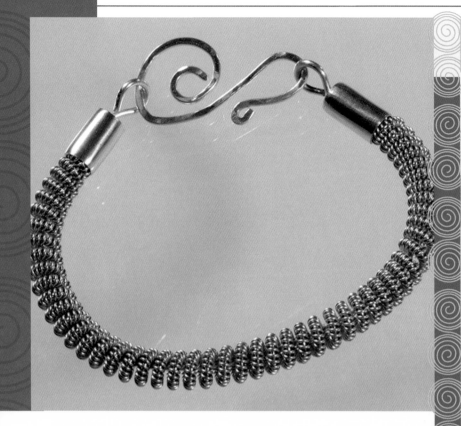

GATHERING YOUR GOODS

16-gauge wire

TOOLS
TO HAVE ON HAND

- Chasing hammer
- Bench block
- Flush cutter
- Round-nose pliers
- Chain-nose pliers

Designer: LeRoy Goertz
Finished Size: 1½" to 2"
Expense: Under $25
Expertise: Beginner

Simple Swan
Clasp

Courtesy of LeRoy Goertz, Coiling Gizmo. Photography by Dave Sharp.

FORMING THE CLASP

STEP A: With 16-gauge wire, make a coil with your round-nose pliers.

STEP B: Grab the wire with chain-nose pliers as shown.

STEP C: Continue coiling. As an option, you can make the hook part by bending the wire with your fingers.

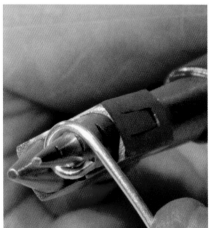

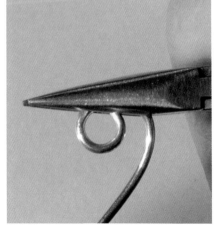

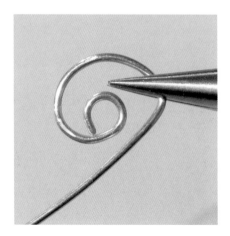

Courtesy of LeRoy Goertz, Coiling Gizmo. Photography by Dave Sharp.

FORMING THE CLASP *continued*

STEP D: Cut the wire with your flush cutter.

Courtesy of LeRoy Goertz, Coiling Gizmo. Photography by Dave Sharp.

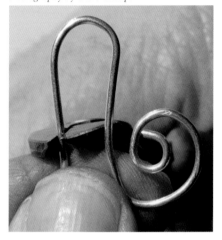

STEP E: Make an eye with the end of your round-nose pliers.

Barbara Markoe: Matahari Bangle Bracelet.

Barbara Markoe: Matahari Silver Bangle Bracelet.

TEXTURING THE CLASP

STEP A: With a bench block and a chasing hammer, place the clasp on the block and hit it repeatedly with the hammer.

Courtesy of LeRoy Goertz, Coiling Gizmo. Photography by Dave Sharp.

STEP B: You can use either the flat side or the ball peen side of the hammer, or a combination of both. Your finished piece will have a wonderful hand-wrought texture to it.

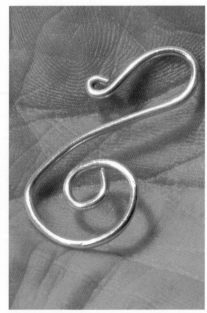

Courtesy of LeRoy Goertz, Coiling Gizmo. Photography by Dave Sharp.

tip

A ball peen hammer has one end of the head that is flat and the other end is shaped like a ball; the "ball peen" side of the hammer is the round ball end of the head.

You can buy special tools that jewelers use, called chasing tools. However, you must be aware that chasing tools are specially made and higher-priced. There are many ordinary tools that can work for making jewelry and they are a lot less expensive than the others.

CHAPTER 8

Coiling by Design

You can coil wire to create multiple looks for all of your jewelry designs, or, follow the instructions to make any of the coiled projects on the following pages.

Courtesy of LeRoy Goertz. Photography by Dave Sharp.

Basic Choker
with Deluxe Gizmo

The Professional Deluxe Coiling Gizmo provides a professional look to your project. Production craftspeople will delight in the speed with which beautiful jewelry can be made.

tip

Longer pieces of wire can be coiled with this technique than with the coil spring technique. The coiling also has a tighter look.

Coiling Wire Directly onto Wire

SETTING UP THE GIZMO

STEP A: Cut a 10" length of 20-gauge wire. Put about 2" of that wire into the chuck and tighten it.

STEP B: Put the end of the wire into one eye of the Gizmo's fishing swivel. Tie the swivel to the tail-stock with a short piece of wire.

One of the features of the Professional Deluxe Coiling Gizmo is that you can coil wire directly onto the mother wire itself. The design of this tool allows you to coil a stretch as long as 30 feet — which should get your imagination going with ideas for creative projects! Remember, when you are coiling, the mother wire must be straight. If it isn't, it will work-harden near where it enters the chuck and break at that point; so always keep it straight.

START COILING THE CHOKER

STEP A: Start the coiling with 24-gauge wire using the directions for making a coil spring on page 84-85. Make about six coils and loosen the chuck.

STEP B: Push the wire into the chuck and clamp it down onto the six coils. Tighten the chuck again, and coil a stretch of wire about 2" long.

STEP C: Unscrew the wing nut on the right side of the black spool.

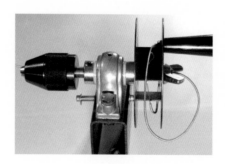

STEP D: Unclamp the tail-stock and move it toward the Gizmo.

STEP E: Loosen the chuck and push the wire into the chuck. It will come out of the hole in the tube that is in the middle of the crank spool.

STEP F: Make a loop out of the bare wire and hook it onto the spool. Then, turn the crank and spool the wire onto the spool.

STEP G: Tighten the chuck and put tension on the long wire by re-clamping the tail-stock.

STEP H: Continue coiling another two feet. Repeat the steps that you just did. You will end up with approximately seven feet of coiled wire.

FINISHING THE CHOKER

STEP A: Make the second coiling around a 10-gauge welding rod as you did for the coil spring bracelet (see page 84-85).

STEP B: Slip the coil off of the welding rod and push a 16-gauge wire into it. Place an end cap onto each end of the choker.

STEP C: Make an eye loop on each end.

STEP D: Wear this piece with the hook at the back of the neck or with the hook in front as a decorative element — your choice!

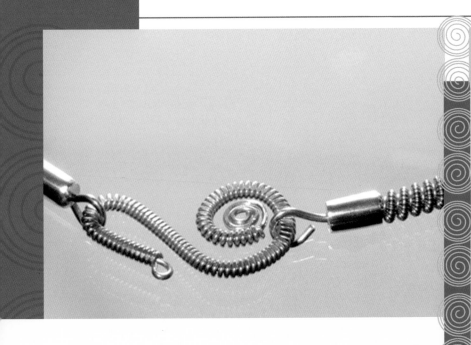

GATHERING
YOUR GOODS

18- and 20-gauge sterling silver wire

TOOLS
TO HAVE ON HAND

- Coiling Gizmo
- Round-nose pliers
- Flush cutter
- 2 bench blocks
- Piece of leather

Designer: LeRoy Goertz
Finished Size: 2" to 3"
Expense: Under $25
Expertise: Intermediate
Time to Complete:
About 15 minutes

Hammered Coiled
Wire Clasp

In this project, you will fashion wire into a hook and hammer it for texture. Concentrate on creating a uniform look.

COILING THE WIRE

STEP A: Insert a 7" length of 18-gauge wire into the chuck of the Gizmo. Push it in about 1½".

STEP B: Coil the 20-gauge wire around the 18-gauge, making the length of coiling about 4". See directions on page 80.

STEP C: Snip off the 20-gauge wire at the end of the coiling. Remove the wire from the chuck and snip off the tail of the wire that was close to the chuck. Take the sharpness off of the snipped wires by working them into the wire with your chain-nose pliers.

SHAPING THE CLASP

STEP A: With your round-nose pliers, make an eye on the bare wire.

STEP B: Continue coiling the wire.

STEP C: With your hand, start to coil the coiled part of the wire and form a Celtic coil. See page 89 for instructions.

STEP D: Make a hook.

FLATTENING THE CLASP

STEP A: Place the clasp on top of one of your bench blocks.

STEP B: Place your second block over the clasp and put a piece of leather on top of the second bench block. Hit it with a hammer. You may have to hit it several times.

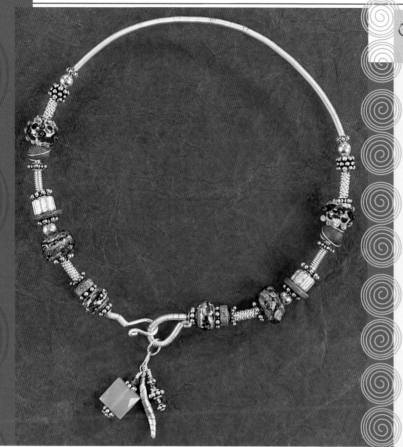

Celestial Bodies

Choker

Keep pre-coiled lengths of various gauge wires on hand so you can cut the size coil you need when assembling your jewelry. This will save you a lot of time!

Approximately 10" of a small gauge wire will make an inch of coil. Use a mandrel size that best reflects the base you will be working on.

GATHERING YOUR GOODS

6	lampwork 10 mm to 15 mm beads
4	sterling silver balls
2	Bali silver 6 mm x 8 mm beads
2	silver 6 mm x 8 mm beads
2	green 8 mm ceramic beads
2	teal 12 mm ceramic spacer discs
2	teal 8 mm ceramic spacer discs
18	Bali silver 6 mm to 12 mm spacer beads, various
19"	14-gauge wire
9	feet 24-gauge wire
4	sterling silver ½" pieces coiled 20-gauge round wire
2	sterling silver ½" pieces twisted 22-gauge wire

For charms

1	green 12 mm x 12 mm faceted chalcedony
3	sapphire 4 mm Indian bicone crystals
1	sterling silver Hilltribe charm
3	sterling silver 24-gauge 2" headpins
6	Bali silver 3 mm to 8 mm spacers
1	Norwegian Bokmal sterling silver 8 mm soldered ring
1	sterling silver 8 mm jump ring

NOTE: Make sure that all beads fit onto 14-gauge wire.

TOOLS TO HAVE ON HAND

- Round-nose pliers
- Chain-nose pliers
- Wire cutters
- Flush cutters
- File (or a fine emery board)
- Chasing hammer
- Steel bench block
- The Coiling Gizmo
- Econo Winder manual

Designer: **Barbara Markoe**

Finished Size: 17", without clasp

MAKING THE CHOKER

When adding beads to bangles, just "go with the flow," although you may choose to lay out your bead design. Each side should measure about 5½" for this project.

STEP A: Start with the 19" piece of 14-gauge wire. This will be your base mandrel. Flatten one end of the wire with a chasing hammer and steel bench block.

STEP B: With the tip of the chain-nose pliers, create a loop at the end where the wire is flat. In the back or largest part of round-nose pliers, form a loop in the opposite direction from the small loop made previously. You now have a hook for your bangle.

STEP C: Using chain-nose pliers, add one or two small bends after the hook. This will help serve as a bead stop.

STEP D: Using the nine feet of 24-gauge wire and the Econo Winder, make a wire coil following the instructions on page 80, Steps A through E.

STEP E: Clip about an inch from the coiled wire. Slip it onto the base mandrel, all the way over small bends up to the hook. The wrap should fit snugly over the bends.

STEP F: Start adding your beads and sections of the coiled wire onto the base mandrel. After the first half of the beads are added, clip 6" from the 24-gauge coiled wire. Add the coil onto the base mandrel. Add remaining set of beads.

STEP G: You should be left with about 1½" to 2" of coiled wire that will form the end loop. If you have NOT pre-designed, then check your balance. Make any spacing adjustments.

STEP H: Flatten the remaining end of the base mandrel with the chasing hammer and steel bench block.

STEP I: Add the remaining 2" of 24-gauge coil. Clip excess coil so the flattened end sticks out about ¼". With the tip of the chain-nose pliers, create a loop at the end where the wire is flat. This should now be holding everything in place. With a large mandrel, finger, or wooden dowel, form a large loop in the opposite direction from the small loop previously made. This is the trickiest part!

STEP J: Adjust the hook and loop so it sits properly on the neck.

STEP K: Using the headpins, string a variety of charms. Wire-wrap them onto the soldered jump ring. Connect this dangle to the large loop with another jump ring.

GATHERING YOUR GOODS

4" to 5" sterling-silver 16-gauge wire

Sterling-silver 20-gauge wire

Bead to accommodate a 16-gauge wire

Piece of leather

TOOLS TO HAVE ON HAND

- Professional Deluxe Coiling Gizmo
- Round-nose pliers
- Flush cutter
- Hammer
- Bench blocks (2)

Designer: LeRoy Goertz
Finished Size: 2" to 3"
Expense: Under $25
Expertise: Intermediate
Time to Complete: 15 to 30 minutes

Clasp
with Wire-Wrapped Bead

Courtesy of LeRoy Goertz, Coiling Gizmo. Photography by Dave Sharp.

WIRE WRAPPING THE BEAD

STEP A: Be sure your bead has a hole that will accommodate a 16-gauge wire.

STEP B: Lay the bead against the 16-gauge wire and cut the wire so that you have 2" of wire on each side of the bead.

STEP C: Place one end of the wire into the Gizmo's chuck and slip the bead onto the wire.

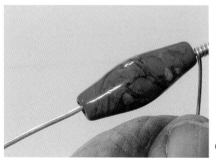

STEP D: Start a coil and make six coils. Coil over the bead and make six coils at the left side of the bead.

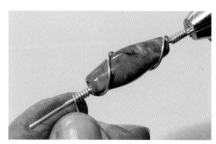

STEP E: Remove the wire from the chuck and snip the wires from each end.

STEP F: The wire may need to be tightened. If so, take your round-nose pliers and make a twist in the wire that goes around the bead.

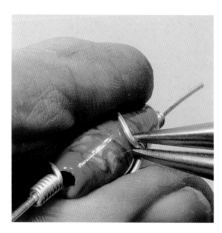

Courtesy of LeRoy Goertz, Coiling Gizmo. Photography by Dave Sharp.

MAKING THE HOOKS

STEP A: Hammer both ends of the wire.

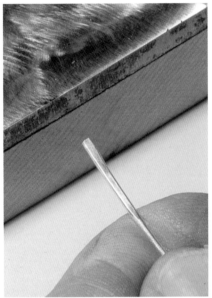

STEP B: Make an eye using the small end of round-nose pliers. Roll the pliers away from you. Repeat on the other end of the bead.

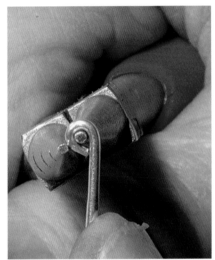

STEP C: Make sure that the wrapped bead is in the center of the wire, and make a bend on each end of the setup.

STEP D: Take the thickest part of the round-nose pliers and roll it toward you to finish the hook. Make a hook on the other end.

Courtesy of LeRoy Goertz, Coiling Gizmo. Photography by Dave Sharp.

HAMMERING THE HOOKS

Place the hook between two bench blocks, and place the leather on top of the second bench block. If you don't want to flatten the eyes, do not put them between the blocks. Hit the leather with a hammer.

The finished clasp.

Now that you have seen how easy the Gizmo makes wire wrapping the beads, why just limit yourself to one bead? Our example below shows a hook with three beads.

Make eyes on both ends of a series of wire-wrapped beads; join the eyes together for a handsome neckpiece.

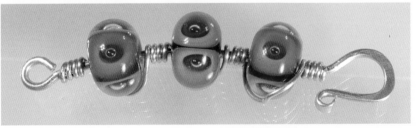

Courtesy of LeRoy Goertz, Coiling Gizmo. Photography by Dave Sharp.

Making a Freeform Bangle Bracelet

STEP A: Flush cut both ends of a 10" piece of 12-gauge wire. A 10" piece of wire will fit about a 7" wrist. Adjust for your size. This is your wire base.

STEP B: With the large end of the round-nose pliers, make a loop or eye on one end of the wire base. Make another loop at the other end.

STEP C: Measure the distance from one loop joint to the next. Measure your focal bead. Subtract the length of your focal bead from the length of the wire base. Divide that number by two. These are the lengths you will be coiling with the Coiling Gizmo or other coiling device.

STEP D: Divide a 36" piece of 20-gauge wire into two equal 18" pieces. With your coiling device and a mandrel the size of the 12-gauge wire, start wrapping one piece of wire, wrapping evenly three or four times to get started. Then, continue in a haphazard way to the length derived in Step C. You should be about half way into the piece of wire. Now, wrap back in the same manner, overlapping the first wrap. When you get to the end of the wire, tuck it in an inconspicuous place.

Use pliers to reach in and squeeze.

STEP E: Remove from the Coiling Gizmo or coiling device and angle-cut the end. Repeat with the other piece of 20-gauge wire. You now have two pieces of coiled wire for your bangle bracelet.

STEP F: Holding the loop end of the wire base, add one spacer bead, one new coil (with the even end next to the spacer) the focal bead, the second coil (with the even side toward the end) and a spacer. You should have enough wire to make a loop and secure the pieces.

STEP G: Divide a 36" piece of 24-gauge wire into two equal pieces. With one piece, start about a third of the way up the base coil on one side, weaving, coiling and adding little silver balls as you go. When you come to the end of the wire, tuck in and hide. With pliers, squeeze to tighten. Repeat for other side.

MAKING THE CLASP

STEP A: Flatten one end of the wire with the chasing hammer and steel bench block.

STEP B: With the tip of the chain-nose pliers, create a loop at the end where the wire is flat.

STEP C: In the back or largest part of the round nose pliers, form a loop in the opposite direction from the small loop made previously.

STEP D: Grasp the other end of the wire with the tip of the round or chain nose pliers. Have as little of the wire peeking through the end of the pliers as possible. Now, begin coiling the wire. Grasping your developing coil with your chain nose pliers, continue to coil until you measure 1⅝" from end to end.

STEP E: Grasp the wire next to coil with chain nose pliers. With your left thumb pressing against the tail of the wire, form a bend. Grasp the loop with large round nose pliers and gently urge the wire to rest next to the coil. Partially close the clasp with the round nose pliers.

STEP F: Use chasing hammer to flatten the curve of loop and also the bend at the bottom of the clasp. Open one eye on bangle and insert clasp through the bottom "V" section. Close the eye.

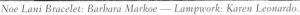

Noe Lani Bracelet: Barbara Markoe — Lampwork: Karen Leonardo.

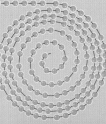
Jump Rings and Assemblage

Courtesy of Beadazzled. Photography by Cas Webber.

Japanese 4-in-1 Bracelet

with Wide Clasp

This bracelet is based on armor worn by the Japanese Samurai that used flexible connections between rigid plates. The spacing of each ring makes it easy to attach beads, findings or just about anything. This pattern is linear, but has great fluidity of movement and allows for a wide variety of jewelry using different ring sizes.

GATHERING YOUR GOODS

Clasp
(with 9 vertical loops)

102 jump rings,
⅛", 18-gauge

63 jump rings ³⁄₁₆",
16-gauge

TOOLS
TO HAVE ON HAND

- Two pairs of flat-nosed pliers
- 12" x 14" piece of dark-colored fabric
- 5 "T" pins
- 12" x 14" foam core board (optional)

Designer: Patrick Ober
Finished Size: 7"
Expense: $25 to $50
Expertise: Intermediate
Time to Complete: An evening

Practice your technique using inexpensive jump rings (copper, NuGold, brass) first, before you work with expensive metals (sterling silver).

CREATE YOUR OWN JUMP RINGS

STEP A: Coil a length of 18- to 22-gauge wire around a mandrel by hand or by using other wire-coiling tools available in craft stores, online or through specialty bead shops.

STEP B: Use wire cutters to cut a complete link from the coil.

STEP C: Close each link tightly when connecting them together or to other portions of a piece you are working on.

Check to see that the gauge of the jump ring is heavy enough to secure attachments.

fix a broken clasp

Broken clasp? You may not need to restring it. Simply place a split ring or jump ring through the loop at the end of the flexible wire next to the crimp. Then, you can safely cut away the broken clasp. Secure the new clasp to the split ring.

STARTING THE CHAIN

Courtesy of Beadazzled. Photography by Cas Webber.

STEP A: Close four ⅛" (small) jump rings and open one ³⁄₁₆" (large) ring. See directions for opening and closing jump rings, page 20.

STEP B: Place the four small closed rings onto the large ring, and then close the large ring.

STEP C: Arrange the rings so that it looks like an "X" with the large ring in the middle.

Each time, after you add a ring, make sure to close it before adding another ring.

BUILDING THE CHAIN

STEP A: Add one large ring onto each small ring.

Courtesy of Beadazzled. Photography by Cas Webber.

STEP B: Attach two small rings onto each of the four large rings that you just added, still trying to keep the "X" arrangement.

STEP C: At the corner of each part of the "X," add one large ring through one small ring from each leg of the "X," making sure not to twist the small rings, or you might lose your pattern. No small rings should be going through another small ring, and the same goes for the large rings.

At this time, try not to pick up your work. Many people like to use "T" pins to hold the work in place.

STEP D: After you have added the large ring that connects each leg of the "X," you should have a little square that has three rows of three large rings, with all of the small rings standing up and all of the large rings lying flat.

EXPANDING THE BRACELET

STEP A: Pick one side of the three-by-three square (usually in the direction of your dominant hand) and add one small ring through one large ring.

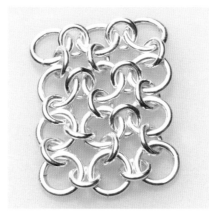

STEP C: Continue to add rows until you have used all of your rings, making a chain 7" long.

STEP B: Attach one large ring to each of the small rings. After the three large rings have been added, use a small ring (two total) to connect each large ring to the next in the row, making little squares.

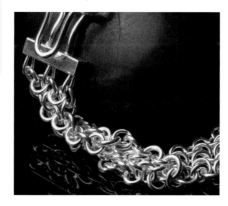

STEP D: Use the last row at each end of the bracelet to add your clasp. Open large rings, one at a time, to hook through the three rings of the clasp to finish off the bracelet.

Courtesy of Beadazzled. Photography by Cas Webber.

tip

1. When making chains, use flat-nosed pliers with narrow tips, — not needle-nosed pliers.

2. Use smooth-jawed pliers so you won't mar or cut your metals.

3. When opening each ring, try not to grip the ring with the pliers so tightly that the pliers mar the rings.

4. Open each ring the same distance, roughly two to three times the thickness of the wire.

5. When opening or closing rings, do not be afraid to discard one that has become damaged or disfigured.

6. When a ring is closed tightly, it will be hard to see the butting of the ends of the rings. The closer and smoother the closure, the less likely for a ring to get caught on anything.

7. Work on a smooth dark-colored piece of fabric (such as Polarfleece), with little nap. It keeps the rings from sliding around and provides contrast to see each step as you are working.

8. Try not to pick up the chain as you make it; the pattern gets confused and mistakes are more likely to happen.

9. Some people like to use "T" pins to hold the work to the fabric so it does not move around. Use a piece of foam core board under your fabric so the "T" pins have a surface to sink into.

10. Experiment with different ring sizes — everyone likes a different look.

11. When your hands or eyes show signs of fatigue, its time to take a break.

1	natural brass 1½" incised setting large fire opal pendant kit*
1	natural brass 8 mm jump ring*
4	natural brass 4.5 mm jump rings*
36	natural brass 4 mm circle spacer beads*
12	natural brass 3 mm cube beads*
12	natural brass 6 mm tube spacer beads*
12	amber 6 mm faceted glass round beads*
2	natural brass 2 mm crimp beads*
20	natural brass 5 mm square filigree bead caps*
3	natural brass 8 mm jump rings*
10	natural brass 4.5 mm jump rings*
1	natural brass ¾" lobster clasp*
13¼"	natural brass 4 mm figaro chain*
18"	bronze 19-strand beading wire*

Vintaj Brass Company, see Resource Guide

TOOLS
TO HAVE ON HAND

- Ergonomic chain-nose pliers (2 pairs)

Designer: Jeanne Holland
Expense: $50 to $75
Expertise: Intermediate
Finished size: 13½"
Time to Complete: An evening

Ancient Hieroglyphic
Fire Opal Choker

SETTING THE STONE

STEP A: Place the loose stone on the setting.

STEP B: Using your left hand, hold the stone in place with your thumb on top of the stone and your first two fingers on the bottom of the setting.

STEP C: Using your right hand, tighten the prongs of the setting with a chain-nose pliers. Position the pliers with one side on the prong and one side underneath the setting. Clamp to tighten.

COMPLETING THE PENDANT

STEP A: Using chain-nose pliers, close your 8 mm jump ring completely. See the basic jump ring technique, page 20.

STEP B: Connect the set stone to the 8 mm jump ring with a 4.5 mm jump ring, using chain-nose pliers.

STEP C: Attach three additional 4.5 mm jump rings to the 8 mm jump ring.

CREATING THE BEADED STRAND

STEP A: String one faceted amber bead and crimp the end.

STEP B: String three circle spacer beads, one cube bead, one tube spacer bead, one square filigree bead cap, one amber faceted bead, and one square filigree bead cap. Repeat four more times.

STEP C: String three circle spacer beads, one cube bead, and one tube spacer bead.

STEP D: String the finished pendant by passing the bead wire through the three 4.5 mm jump rings attached to the pendant.

STEP E: Repeat steps B and A in reverse.

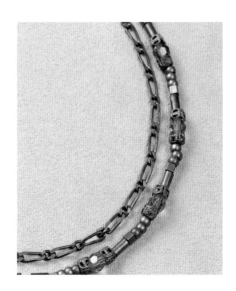

ASSEMBLING THE NECKLACE

STEP A: Attach the beaded strand to the chain length using an 8 mm jump ring at each end.

STEP B: Attach one 4.5 mm jump ring to the 8 mm jump ring on the right end of the necklace.

STEP C: Attach the lobster clasp to the 4.5 mm jump ring on the right end of the necklace using another 4.5 mm jump ring. Your necklace is complete!

GATHERING
YOUR GOODS

4   natural brass 17 mm
        multi-strand necklace
        connectors*

6   natural brass 17 mm
        deco two-hole
        connectors*

6   natural brass 4.5 mm
        jump rings*

* Vintaj Natural Brass Company.
   see Resource Guide

TOOLS
TO HAVE ON HAND

- Rosary pliers
  with side cutter
- Chain-nose pliers
  (2 pairs)

Double-Sided Connectors

with *Jeanne Holland*

Designer: **Jeanne Holland**
Flower Filigree Necklace

Creating double-sided connectors will add variety, weight and versatility to your designs.

LAYING OUT THE COMPONENTS

STEP A: Lay out two sets of multi-strand connectors layered back to back, with the widest part facing each other.

STEP B: Line up your deco connectors, layered back to back, between the sets of multi-strand connectors. Line up one set of deco connectors with each of the outermost holes and one set with the center holes.

ASSEMBLING THE CONNECTOR SECTION

Using 4.5 mm jump rings; attach the connectors in the order they are laid out. See the basic jump ring technique, page 20.

GATHERING YOUR GOODS

3	mottled aqua and amber 20 mm handmade glass lentil beads
1	natural brass 5 mm dimple bead*
1	amber 6 mm faceted glass round
6	natural brass 8 mm ornate bead caps*
2	natural brass 6 mm scalloped bead caps*
16	natural brass 17 mm multi-strand connectors*
28	natural brass 17 mm deco two-hole connectors*
1	natural brass ¾" filigree clasp*
1½"	natural brass 3 mm ladder chain*
3	natural brass 1½" eyepins*
1	natural brass 1" headpin*
37	natural brass 4.5 mm jump rings*

*Vintag Natural Brass Co., see Resource Guide.

Briny Deep
Choker

CREATING THE BEAD LINKS

STEP A: Create links by stringing one ornate bead cap, one lentil bead, and one ornate bead cap on a 1½" eyepin.

STEP B: Push the bead caps securely against the beads.

STEP C: Create three links in total.

TOOLS TO HAVE ON HAND

- Rosary pliers with side cutter
- Chain-nose pliers (2 pairs)

Designer: Jeanne Holland
Finished Size: Adjustable 14" to 16"
Expense: Under $25
Expertise: Beginner
Time to Complete: An evening

MAKING THE CONNECTOR SECTIONS

Create four connector sections. See Assemblage below.

CREATING THE NECKLACE EXTENDER

STEP A: Create a beaded drop by stringing one dimple bead, one scalloped bead cap, one amber faceted round and one scalloped bead cap on a 1" headpin.

STEP B: Place your round-nose pliers ¼" from your last bead. Using your thumb and forefinger, bend the wire over the back of your pliers.

STEP C: Cross the wire underneath and in front of the stationary wire, forming the start of a loop.

STEP D: Attach your beaded drop to your 1½" section of ladder chain using a 4.5 mm jump ring. See the basic jump ring technique, page 20.

ASSEMBLING THE NECKLACE

Link the following using 4.5 mm jump rings between each component: necklace extender, two deco connectors layered back to back, connector section, bead link, connector section, bead link, connector section, bead link, connector section, two deco connectors layered back to back, and one filigree clasp.

HERE'S HOW TO ASSEMBLE BEADED PORTIONS WITH FILIGREE EMBELLISHMENTS:

STEP A: Lay out the items you will need: beads, bead caps, eyepins, jump rings and filigree connectors.

STEP B: Assemble bead components using eyepins, beads, and bead caps. Connect to filigree embellishment with jump rings.

STEP C: This makes the beginning of off-shoots for your design.

Glossary

See more jewelry making definitions at www.wigjig.com.

Anvil

A hard metal tool used as the base when hammering wire. Similar to a blacksmith's anvil in shape, but significantly smaller, anvils are often used with a chasing hammer to harden jewelry wire components and can be used to flatten wire.

Artistic Wire

Manufacturer of wire used for craft projects and for making jewelry. Artistic Wire makes silver-plated, brightly-colored wire, vinyl-coated copper-colored wire, and natural copper and brass wire. By using enamel or vinyl coatings on the wire, many types of Artistic Wire will not tarnish with normal wear and tear.

Beadalon

Brand of stainless-steel bead-stringing wire, made of multiple threads of stainless steel coated with plastic to preserve the stainless steel.

Bead cap

A decorative cover, usually made of metal, for the top or bottom of a bead.

Bead dangle

A combination of one or more beads on a head pin that has been shaped to allow the bead or beads to hang from a loop at the top.

Bead-stringing wire

Highly-flexible, multi-stranded stainless-steel wire used for stringing beads. These wire products are resistant to breaking due to the sawing action of the beads on the stringing material.

Bench block

A tool used to provide a hard flat surface for hammering wire; a bench block is normally a square shaped piece of hardened steel.

Bent chain-nose pliers

Pliers that have flat smooth jaws, but the jaws are bent. This facilitates keeping your wrist straight while you grip your jewelry project.

Bezel

A setting that holds a gemstone. The face of the gemstone is encircled by the setting and held in place from the back. Because the setting holds the entire face of the gemstone, bezel type settings are generally very secure. Unfortunately, bezel settings tend to make the gemstone appear smaller, as opposed to the Tiffany and other prong type settings where the entire gemstone is visible.

Bicone

A shape of bead faceted to reflect more light.

Brass

A yellow metal alloy frequently made of about 55-65 percent copper and between 37-45 percent zinc. It is a soft metal and is suitable for casting and making jewelry wire.

Bugle beads

Small cylindrical beads, they are frequently either 2 mm wide by 4 mm long or 2 mm wide by 7 mm long.

Bur cup

A tool used to remove the burs or sharp corners or residue on the end of a cut piece of wire.

Chain-nose pliers

Pliers with straight, tapered jaws and a flat, smooth, inner surface; they are used for grasping and holding wire while minimizing the marks left on the wire.

Chasing hammer

A special type of hammer made with a very smooth, flat face to hammer and flatten wire. Hammering the wire is frequently used to harden the wire. The smooth flat face minimizes the marking of the wire while hammering.

Copper

The 29th element in the periodic table of elements, this soft metal conducts heat and electricity very well. It is frequently drawn into wire that is used for electrical conductors or for making jewelry.

Crimp/crimping

The process of squeezing small crimp beads to hold bead-stringing thread or wire. Often, loops in the bead-stringing material are made by passing the stringing material through the crimp bead, then through a finding, like a clasp, and finally back through the crimp bead. The crimped bead connects the bead-stringing material to the clasp with a permanent connection.

Crystal

A higher grade of glass with added lead. The lead adds both brilliance (light reflectivity) and strength.

Crystal pearls

Simulated pearl beads made by Swarovski. They are among the best quality of the artificial pearls. The core of a Crystal Pearl bead is crystal glass. The outside is a simulated pearl coating.

Cup bur

Tool used to remove the burs or small imperfections on the end of a cut wire segment. The cup bur has a small cup that had diamond dust glued to the inside to act as the abrasive agent that in effect removes the burs on the wire leaving a smooth, rounded end. This process is very important when making ear wires.

Curb (chain)

The curb style of chain is a way of making a chain with twisted links so that the chain will lie flat.

Dichroic (glass beads)

Dichroic, as it refers to a type of glass, can have two or more colors in the glass.

Dowel

A rod generally used for wrapping wire around to create coils of wire. Also called a mandrel.

Drop or Dangle

Decorative wire component frequently used to make earrings.

Ear clip

A type of ear wire finding, an ear clip is made of two or more components held in the closed position by a spring.

Ear clutch

Metal or plastic component used to hold a post style of ear wire on the wearer's ear. It slides on the post and is held in place by friction.

Ear wire

A finding used to allow the wearing of earrings. The ear wire connects the earring body to the wearer's ear.

End cap

A finding used to cover the ends of wire. End caps have a hole drilled ½ of the way through the metal ball and are glued on the end of the wire

Eye loop

A special type of loop where the loop is centered above the remainder of the wire segment.

Eye pin

Similar to a head pin, an eye pin has an eye loop on the end of a straight wire segment.

Figaro (chain)

A style of curb chain that uses both large and small links combined to make the chain. The links are twisted in the curb style so that the chain will lie flat.

Figure-eight connector

A wire component made of two loops back-to-back. The resulting wire is in the shape of the number eight and can be used to connect wire components, one in each loop.

Finding

A jewelry-making component, frequently made of metal. Ear wires, head pins, eye pins and clasps are examples of findings.

Fine silver

An alloy of silver made of pure silver with the remainder being trace impurities.

Fire polished

A less expensive way of polishing cut glass, in this process heat is used to smooth the outer surface of the cut glass. In general, fire-polished beads are faceted. Many fire-polished beads are made in the Czech Republic.

Fine step-jaw pliers

A type of step-jaw pliers made specifically to work with the WigJig family of tools. The initial step in these pliers makes a loop the size of the pegs for the WigJig Delphi, Cyclops or Centaur. The second loop in these pliers makes a loop the size of the pegs for the WigJig Olympus, Olympus-Lite or Electra. The third loop makes a loop 9/64" in diameter. Because these pliers have a flat jaw, and the round, stepped jaw, they do not mark the outside of the loop of wire that is made.

Flush cutter

A jewelry wire cutter made to cut wire, leaving one side of the cut to be flush (or flat) and the other side of the cut to be sharp (pointed). A conventional cutter will cut the wire leaving both sides semi-sharp. One side of the jaws is flat, the opposite side is beveled.

French ear wire

Also called a shepherd's hook, this ear wire finding is commonly used.

Glass

Generally, a silica compound combined with boric oxide, aluminum oxide or phosphorus pentoxide. By using heat, glass can be formed into many shapes and is used extensively in the manufacture of beads.

Glass pearls

Simulated pearls made from adding a pearl-like coating onto a glass bead.

Gold

The 79th element in the periodic table of elements, gold is a corrosion resistant element and for this reason is used frequently in more expensive jewelry. Because gold is relatively rare, it is considered to be valuable.

Gold-filled

The process of physically combining a thin alloy of gold with a gold-tone base metal, the base metal adds strength and is fabricated, so that it is on the inside of the wire or sheet metal. The gold alloy on the outside provides the color, corrosion resistance and permanence of real gold. The combination of the gold alloy on the outside and the gold-tone metal, on the inside where it can not be seen, allows jewelry designers to make gold-filled jewelry at a fraction of the cost of solid gold, but with the look and feel of solid gold. Most gold-filled wire is made of 5 percent gold alloy and the remainder is gold tone metal.

Gold-plated

An electro-chemical process of coating a conductive metal wire with a very thin layer of 24-carat gold. The layer of gold in the plating is one to two molecules of gold thick. Over time, this thin layer of gold can be worn off by abrasion, making gold-plating best used in items that receive limited wear and tear.

Griffin

A brand of bead-stringing thread made of silk or nylon.

Half-hard

High quality wire can be made in a variety of hardnesses from dead soft to full hardened. In the middle of this range is wire hardness called half hard. This wire is stiffer than dead-soft wire and not as stiff and springy as fully hardened wire. In general, only gold, gold-filled, sterling silver and fine silver wire can be purchased with a hardness of ½ hard.

Hank

Strands of beads grouped together. Frequently, seed beads are sold by the hank.

Hard wire

Hard wire is the stiffest, least easy to bend and most springy of all the wire hardnesses. This type of wire is not used a great deal because it is difficult to bend.

Harden

The process of making a jewelry component more stiff and permanent can be accomplished in a variety of ways, including hammering and work hardening.

Hardness

The property of how easy or how hard it is to bend the wire. Soft wire is very easy to bend. Hard wire is stiff and springy.

Head pin

Finding with a flat head on one end and straight wire on the other end, head pins are used to make bead dangles and attach beads to loops for jewelry.

Hemostat

Medical tool that is a type of clamp that's easy to close with one hand and remain closed. In making jewelry, hemostats are frequently used to hold the end of thread or flexible wire while you are adding beads to a necklace or bracelet.

Jeweler's block

Same as a bench block

Jewelry wire

Jewelry wire can be brass, copper, gold, sterling silver, fine silver, gold-filled and/or gold- and silver-plated wire.

Jig

Jewelry making tool with a series of pegs used to form or shape wire.

Jump ring

Metal finding that is round and can be opened to use as a connector, or they can be soldered closed.

Lampwork beads

Handmade beads created by melting glass on a mandrel and shaping the bead. The resulting beads can have many different colors of glass and a unique shape. Lampwork beads are, in general, more expensive since they are usually handmade.

Lobster-claw clasp

Clasp with the shape of a lobster's claw.

Loop

Circle made in a wire segment.

Magnetic beads

Metallic beads made of a magnetic material. The beads can be dark in color, or they can be made with a silver or gold plating. Some semi-precious gemstones, like hematite, can have natural magnetism.

Magnetic clasp

Jewelry finding made of a pair of magnets with silver, silver-plated, gold, gold-plated or gold-filled cover glued over the magnets. The magnetic property of attraction causes the clasp to stay closed. Tugging gently to overcome the magnetism will open the clasp.

Master coiler

Type of step-jaw pliers that supports making loops in the wire, while minimizing the marks on the wire. They also enable making loops in one of three very consistent sizes.

Memory wire

Wire that is hardened and made in a round shape. The hardening preserves the round shape and makes this wire excellent to use for making either beaded necklaces or bracelets. The memory in the name of this wire refers to the property of the metal to return to its memory-programmed shape.

Nylon

Synthetic material used to make thread for stringing beads. Nylon is strong and can be dyed a variety of colors.

Nylon jaw pliers

Pliers with jaws made of nylon, are softer on jewelry wire, and for this reason, the nylon will not scratch or mark the jewelry wire. These pliers are often used to straighten wire and to squeeze wire components to flatten and harden them.

Nymo

Brand of bead-stringing thread made of nylon.

Open loop

Jewelry-making technique using chain nose or bent chain-nose pliers to open a loop without distorting the shape. By opening a loop, you can connect other components to this loop, and then close the loop, while retaining the round shape of the loop. See page XX.

"P" loop

A loop made with wire where the loop is on one side of the wire. The shape of the loop and the wire makes this look like the letter "P", hence the name.

Pliers

Hand tools used for bending, grasping or shaping wire.

Pony beads

Beads that are generally cylindrical in shape with a larger hole.

Polishing

The process of smoothing the surface of an object. With jewelry, wire polishing results in a shiny appearance and can remove minor tool marks or blemishes. Frequently, polishing involves using a mildly abrasive polishing compound to remove a thin layer of material.

Pressed glass (beads)

A technique for making glass beads, this technique involves shaping heated glass in a mold to create beads. Because of the process for making pressed glass, these beads tend to have a rounded shape and are less expensive than cut glass beads.

Rattail

Bead-stringing cord, generally made of satin. This cord is larger than thread and is used with beads with a larger hole.

Reamers

Jewelry-making tools used to enlarge the size of the hole in a bead, by placing the reamer bit into the hole in the bead, and spinning the bit. The abrasive nature of the bit removes some of the bead material causing the existing hole to become larger.

Ribbon

Fabric-based bead-stringing material.

Rondelle

A shape of bead essentially shaped like a Life Saver candy.

Round (beads):

Spherical shaped beads, round beads may be faceted or may be smooth like a pearl.

Round-nose pliers

Pliers with two conical jaws. They are used for making loops. The size of the loop made is determined by how far down the jaws the loop is made. Loops made near the tips are smaller; loops made near the hinge are larger.

Round (wire):

Wire with a round cross section.

Seed bead

A type of small bead, seed beads are often made of colored glass and are inexpensive. These beads range in size from 1 mm thick to less than 3 mm in thickness.

Silamide Nylon

A brand of nylon bead-stringing thread.

Silk

A type of bead-stringing thread. Historically, quality necklaces were strung on silk. At present, there are many alternatives to silk that are stronger and equally as colorful.

Silver

Element number 47 from the periodic chart of the elements, silver has outstanding ability to conduct heat and electricity. It is used in making jewelry because of its ability to be polished to a shiny surface.

Soft Touch

A premium brand of stainless-steel, bead-stringing wire made by the Soft Flex Company. It is more flexible and supple than Soft Flex, but retains the same strength.

Spiral (in wire)

Wire component made by wrapping wire around itself in a flat plane. Spirals can only be made in wire with a hardness of dead soft.

Spiral Maker

The WigJig Spiral Maker is an accessory that when used with an associated WigJig jig, helps to make spirals without marking the wire. The spiral is made between the Spiral Maker and the jig, and since both are relatively soft plastic, they do not mark the wire.

Split ring

A circular finding made of hardened wire. The wire is wrapped in a circle about 1½ times so that there is overlap. The hardening of the wire preserves the shape of the split ring as it is used to connect other components.

Split-ring pliers

Special pliers used to hold a split ring open so that other components can be connected to the ring.

Spool knitter

Tool used to support making knitted wire chains.

Spring-ring clasp

A type of clasp made in the shape of a ring. A segment of the ring can be withdrawn into the ring to allow connecting the clasp to a loop. The spring in the sliding segment causes the ring to close once pressure is removed.

Sterling silver

A very common alloy of silver made of 92.5 percent pure silver and 7.5 percent copper.

Straightening wire

The technique for removing the curl in wire, leaving it straight. Both the manufacturing process and packaging of wire tend to make the wire have a natural curl. For this reason, straightening the wire is the first step in most jewelry-making projects. Pulling the wire through the jaws of nylon-jaw pliers will straighten the wire.

Stretch Magic

A synthetic bead-stringing material similar to elastic that has the ability to stretch. For this reason, it is used to make beaded bracelets that do not require a clasp. The bracelet can stretch over the wearer's hand.

Super Pegs

A WigJig accessory that facilitates making rounded shapes in wire. The Super Pegs are shaped like a mushroom. The stem of the mushroom fits into the hole in the jig and the top of the mushroom allows making round wire shapes.

Teardrop (beads)

A shape of bead similar to an upside-down pear.

Toggle clasp

Type of clasp that has a bar and a large loop. When worn, the bar is fitted into the loop.

Tube (beads)

Shape of beads that are long, relatively thin, cylinders.

Tweezers

A hand tool used to grasp and hold small objects like beads or bead-stringing thread.

Twist 'n' Curl

Tool used for making wire beads that consist of a handle and a central rod. The wire is wound onto the mandrel to make long coils, which are wound on the rod again to make wire beads. Coiling Gizmo, the trade marked brandname product used for coiling wire by using a chuck, a hollow shaft and a crank. Please note, there are other manufacturers who make other tools to accomplish this task.

Twisting tools

Tools used to make wire beads.

WigJig

The trademarked brand name product used for making jigs for jewelry making. The jigs provide a matrix of holes in a clear acrylic base that allow positioning of metal pegs to make jewelry components Please note, there are many manufacturers who make jewelry-making jigs.

Work hardening

The process of making jewelry components more permanent and stiffer (hardening) by flexing the component repeatedly. This can be accomplished with your fingers or with nylon jaw pliers. Work hardening is accomplished by the initial shaping of the wire with pliers and/or a jewelry-making jig.

Wrapped bead link

A technique using your round nose pliers and bent chain-nose pliers, one or more beads, and some wire. The link is used to connect wire components, sections of commercial chain, or other wrapped bead links. Because the ends of the link are wrapped closed, this link is very strong.

Yoke

The centerpiece in a necklace.

Index

E

F

G

H

I

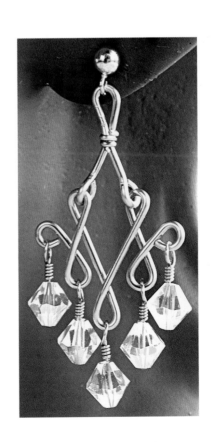

N

O

P

R

S

X

Contributors

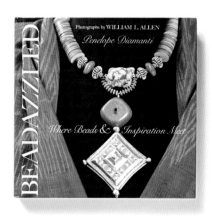

ABOUT THE PHOTOGRAPHER: WILLIAM ALLEN

Photographer William L. (Bill) Allen served as the Editor-in-Chief of National Geographic for ten years. During his 35-year career he covered the world producing hundreds of magazine articles and books as a photographer, writer, or editor on topics ranging from the discovery of the Titanic to 21st Century slavery. Under his leadership, the magazine earned numerous top magazine awards and dealt with important topics such as weapons of mass destruction, global warming, and the public controversy over evolution.

He continues his interest in world cultures and photography through photography of beads and artwork, as well as teaching digital photography and creativity at photography workshops. More information is available at his Web site, www. billallenphotography.com.

ABOUT THE PHOTOGRAPHER: CAS WEBBER

Over the last 20 years Cas has been living and working in Baltimore City. She earned a BFA in Photography & Performing Arts in 1992, and found that creative diversity and freedom have been her life's passion. Whether she is building for a props and sets company, custom painting, rehabbing her house, teaching jewelry, designing jewelry, shooting commercially, managing Baltimore's Beadazzled, or traveling for beads, she is always involved in a creative endeavor. Her current assignments have focused on expanding her photography career while collaborating with various businesses and craftspeople to visually introduce their products and brand their style in the marketplace.

About the Author

SUSAN RAY

Susan Ray has more than 30 years of experience in the fashion and craft industry as author, buyer, merchandise manager, vice president of product and Web site development, including: Peck & Peck and Frederick Atkins of New York, Ben Franklin Retail Stores and JoAnn's Fabrics', Ideaforest Web site. She has spent years traveling to the Far East to develop proprietary products for many retailers throughout the country.

The strength of Susan's entrepreneurial spirit has attracted many companies to utilize her expertise in formulating new store concepts. She was co-founder of a group of award-winning children's computer exploration facilities which received a ComputerWorld Smithsonian Award for heroic innovation of technology.

Susan now lives with her husband, Kevin Duhme, on their dairy farm in Maquoketa, Iowa. Susan Ray is co-author of *The Art and Soul of Glass Beads*, the author of *Easy Beaded Jewelry, Organic Beaded Jewelry*, and *Beaded Jewelry: The Complete Guide*, by Krause Publications. In recent years, she has celebrated the marriage of her son, Eric, to his wife, Velvette, who now shares Susan's passion for beading. Susan's jewelry, craft and interior designs have been featured in numerous national publications, including *Better Homes and Gardens* and *Woman's Day* magazines.

Designer Susan Ray. Lampwork beads by Karen Leonardo.

Resource Guide

Recommended Suppliers:

Artistic Wire
752 North Larch Avenue
Elmhurst, IL 60126
630.530.7567
630.530.7536
sales@artisticwire.com

Ashes to Beauty Adornments
115 Camino de las Huertas
Placitas, NM 87043
505.867.4244

Beadazzled
1507 Connecticut Ave., NW
Washington, D.C.
202.265.2323
www.beadazzled.net

Cas Webber Photography
CasWebber@mac.com
www.caswebber.com

Galena Beads "serving creativity"
109 N. Main Street
Galena, IL 61036
815.777.4080
www.galenabeads.com

Fire Mountain Gems
One Fire Mountain Way
Grants Pass, OR 97526
800.423.2319
Email: questions@firemtn.com
www.firemountaingems.com

Judikins, Inc.
Judi Watanabe
17803 S. Harvard Blvd.
Gardena, CA 90248
310.515.1115
Email: customerservice@judikins.comwww.
judikins.com

Just Leonardo
www.leonardolampwork.com
Karen Leonardo
362 Hood School Road
Indiana, PA 15701
724.357.8709
eBay ID: justleonardo

The Coiling Gizmo/The Refiner's Fire
P.O. Box 66612
Portland, OR 97290
503.775.5242
Fax: 503.774.5448
sales@coilinggizmo.com
www.coilinggizmo.com

Rio Grande (wholesale only)
7500 Bluewater Road, NW
Albuquerque, NM 87121
800.253.9738
Email: info@riogrande.com
www.riogrande.com

Sandra Webster Jewelry
5217 Old Spicewood Spg. Rd. #2003
Austin, TX 78731
512.794.9335
rwebster1@austin.rr.com
www.sandrawebsterjewelry.com

School of Beadwork
P.O. Box 4625
San Luis Obispo, CA 93403
805.440.2613
info@schoolofbeadwork.com
www.schoolofbeadwork.com

Vintaj Natural Brass Co.
P.O. Box 246
Galena, IL 61036
815.541.5558
Email: Jeanne@vintaj.com
www.vintaj.com

WigJig
P.O. Box 5124
Gaithersburg, MD 20882
800.579.WIRE
custsrv@wigjig.com
www.wigjig.com

Contributors

William L. Allen
P.O. Box 7410
Alexandria, VA 22307
202.374.3939
allenngs@earthlink.net

Ilene Baranowitz
1953 Lake Brook Circle
Dandridge, TN 37725
865.397.3880
ibaran@comcast.net

Sherrie Chapin
Blue Moon Jewelry
White Bear Lake, MN
651.503.5820
mail@bluemoonjewelry.com
www.bluemoonjewelry.com

Penelope Diamanti
Beadazzled, Inc.
1507 Connecticut Ave., NW
Washington, D.C.
202.265.2323
www.beadazzled.net

Leroy Goertz
The Refiner's Fire
P.O. Box 66612
Portland, OR 97290
503.775.5242
info@coilinggizmo.com
www.leroygoertz.com

Gary L. Helwig
WigJig
P.O. Box 5124
Gaithersburg, MD 20882
800.579.WIRE
custsrv@wigjig.com
www.wigjig.com

Jeanne Holland
Vintaj Natural Brass Co.
P.O. Box 246
Galena, IL 61036
815.541.5558
Jeanne@vintaj.com
www.vintaj.com

Susan Karczewski
Purr-fectly Unique Jewelry
1112 Brubaker Street
Warsaw, IN 46580
574.268.1110
purrjewelry@comcast.net

Jan Ketza-Harris
Galena Beads "serving creativity"
109 N. Main Street
Galena, IL 61036
815.777.4080
www.galenabeads.com

Jessica Italia
Galena Beads "serving creativity"
109 N. Main Street
Galena, IL 61036
815.777.4080
www.galenabeads.com

Trish Italia
Galena Beads "serving creativity"
109 N. Main Street
Galena, IL 61036
815.777.4080
www.galenabeads.com

Darien Kaiser
7112 Pine Rd.
East Dubuque, IL 61025
815.747.8821
dkaiser@yousq.net

Deanna R. Killackey
1N526 Creekside Court
Lombard, IL 60148
630.336.9754
d_deluco@yahoo.com

Janet L. Killackey
3826 Saltmeadow Court South
Jacksonville, FL 32224
904.992.7293
jkillack@comast.net

Sue Kwong and Karen Li
2310 S. 8th Avenue
Arcadia, CA 91006
616.574.3186
heartbeads@adelphia.net

Dotsie S. Mack
Beadazzled, Inc.
501 N. Charles St.
Baltimore, MD 21201
410.837.2323
dot.mack@mac.com

Kathleen P. Manning
Beadazzled, Inc.
1507 Connecticut Avenue, NW
Washington, DC 20036
202.265.2323

Barbara Markoe
Rituals Jewelry
10668 Ranch Road
Culver City, CA 90230
310.202.7807
ritualsjewelry@comcast.net
www.ritualsjewelry.com

MacKenzie Mullane
Mac Mullane
P.O. Box 246
Galena, IL 61036
815.541.0219
mac@vintaj.com
www.macmullane.com

Wendy Mullane
Vintaj Natural Brass Co.
P.O. Box 246
Galena, IL 61036
815.541.0219
wendy@vintaj.com
www.vintaj.com

Patrick Ober
Patrick Ober Chainmail Armour of Jewelry
150 Main Street
Felton, PA 17322
717.246.8674
armourer@earthlink.net

Susan Ray
Bead A Simple Life
North Fork Farms
18098 Fulton Road
Maquoketa, IA 52060
563.652.3307
raysa524@aol.com
www.beadasimplelife.com

Cathie Roberts
Galena Beads "serving creativity"
109 N. Main Street
Galena, IL 61036
815.777.4080
www.galenabeads.com

Ronda Terry
Terry's Treasures
586.943.5400
Ronda@rondaterry.com
www.rondaterry.com

Sandra Webster
Sandra Webster Jewelry
5217 Old Spicewood Spg. Rd. #2003
Austin, TX 78731
512.794.9335
rwebster1@austin.rr.com
www.sandrawebsterjewelry.com

Cindy Yost & Kat Allison
Guppy Sisters
111 Fischer Drive
Newport News, VA 23602
757.875.5156
copperleaf@cox.net
www.beadworkzstore.com
www.copperloom.com

Discover Beautiful Beaded Ingenuity

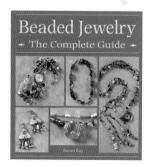